The Revd Canon Graham B. Ushe
Northumberland. Prior to ordina
and now serves as a Secretary of State appointee in the Northumberland National Park Authority, and also as Chairman of the North East Regional Advisory Committee of the Forestry Commission. He has contributed to *Faith and the Future of the Countryside*, edited by Jill Hopkinson and Alan Smith (Canterbury Press, 2012).

PLACES OF ENCHANTMENT

Meeting God in landscapes

Graham B. Usher

Illustrations by M. J. Forster

First published in Great Britain in 2012

Society for Promoting Christian Knowledge
36 Causton Street
London SW1P 4ST
www.spckpublishing.co.uk

British Library Cataloguing-in-Publication Data
A catalogue record for this book is available from the British Library

ISBN 978–0–281–06792–3
eBook ISBN 978–0–281–06793–0

Typeset by Graphicraft Limited, Hong Kong
First printed in Great Britain by Ashford Colour Press
Subsequently digitally printed in Great Britain

Produced on paper from sustainable forests

For Chad and Olivia,
and in memory of their grandfather,
Kenneth Thomson,
and his 'unequivocal yes'

And I felt
a presence that disturbs me with the joy
of elevated thoughts; a sense sublime
of something far more deeply infused,
whose dwelling is the light of setting suns,
and the round ocean, and the living air,
and the blue sky, and in the mind of man,
a motion and a spirit, that impels
all thinking things, all objects of all thought,
and rolls through all things.

William Wordsworth (1770–1850),
'Lines composed a few miles above
Tintern Abbey', 1798

Contents

———•◆•———

Acknowledgements

It is a pleasure to thank those whose support and encouragement have made this book possible: Martin Wharton, Bishop of Newcastle, for granting me a period of sabbatical study leave in which to visit National Parks in California, to travel in the Amazon basin, and to have time to write; Saulo de Barros, Bishop of the Amazon, his wife Ruth, and their community; Sérgio Silva for translating community meetings and discussions in Amazonian villages; sabbatical travel grants from the Diocese of Newcastle, Ecclesiastical Insurance Group's Clergy Bursary Scheme, USPG's Expanding Horizons Programme, Hexham Abbey Parochial Church Council and the Worshipful Company of Mercers, the Abbey's co-patrons; my clergy colleagues, Joanna Anderson and Alan Currie, together with Hexham Abbey's heavenly host of retired clergy, and its staff team, Churchwardens and congregation; staff at the Forestry Commission including Tim Rollinson, Brendan Callaghan and Isabel Farries; staff and members at Northumberland National Park Authority, particularly Tony Gates; Robin Dower for help about his great uncle G. M. Trevelyan; Denise Inge for guidance about Thomas Traherne; for reference details, Kathleen Deignan and Christine M. Bochen regarding Thomas Merton, Helen Hyland at the National Gallery of Australia, and Helen Fordham at St Alban's Cathedral; staff of the British Library and the National Library of Scotland who have been helpful with my enquiries; David Wilbourne and Dagmar Winter for reading and commenting on parts of the manuscript, though any remaining errors are entirely my own fault; and Alison Barr at SPCK for her support with this project.

Acknowledgements

I would especially like to thank my wife Rachel, and our children, Chad and Olivia, who as well as sharing in the journey of writing this book, are companions on many walks and adventures in landscapes that, more often than not, leave us inspired and thankful.

Introduction

For many people God is not encountered in church buildings, nor in musical settings sung by a robed choir, or even in a carefully planned liturgy. For them, all that seems too restrictive, hemmed in and packaged. However, walk with them into a beautiful landscape and they speak of encountering God in the wonder of the scenery. This book seeks to explore why landscapes are spiritually important for people and why landscapes may continue to be the arena for revelation about God.

Getting out into a landscape is good for our overall health. The National Trust markets its properties on city-centre billboards with the slogan 'Getting back to nature is time well spent', and its website encourages, 'Escape the daily hustle and bustle and head into the outdoors – the perfect place to refresh both the body and soul.'[1] Why is it that we exclaim, 'What a view!' or 'Wow, this is heavenly', see our garden as 'my little piece of paradise', or sense the presence of God somehow there in a landscape in front of us? How is it that in these landscapes God seizes our imagination? It is as if heaven is open to earth and earth is open to heaven, the seen world glimpsing the unseen, and we realize that we are more than just the words we speak and the things we think. Though the opposite can also be true, we have a sense, for perhaps just a fleeting moment, that any distance between ourselves and God is taken away. For that precious instant the earth is a veritable theophany full of the grandeur of God, and everything is bursting forth with God's promise and glory.

Turn the pages of Scripture and you find the divine drama unfolding through the beauty of a garden, between the rocky pinnacles of a mountain, by the coolness of the riverside, in the harsh parched wilderness, and among the turmoil and busyness of a crowded city. Down the centuries a host of seekers and sojourners, poets and pilgrims have sought out these places, often finding God's presence in unexpected ways. Painters have captured in strokes on canvas something of the numinous they see before them. Chroniclers have etched the way that the aesthetic has changed them. Writers have tried to describe the power that these places play on the imagination. Many of the world's saints went to extreme measures to live deep within a landscape, whether that be in the Egyptian desert or in the squalor of a slum, so that the heartbeat of God in that place might become their own. Even the idyllic scenes from British landscapes, complete with typical weather, form the backdrop for each page of my new passport. It seems that landscape seeps into our identity and helps to make us who we are.

Many of my own memories tie faith with landscape. Long walks in the woods of Morayshire in the north of Scotland with my Presbyterian grandfather, where stories of the Bible were taught to me and seemed to fit the contours of the ground we walked on. Standing on a hillock overlooking the sea on Anglesey as a 16-year-old, the warm wind in my face, and somehow for the first real time saying 'yes' to the God who I had questioned and tried to fathom from different directions as a teenager. Being scared witless traversing the Aonach Eagach ridge as a student, along the north side of Glencoe, in thick ice and coming up close to the fact that I could easily be dead. Delighting in the warmth of the evening sun as it slipped below the rolling pastures of a Shropshire vista, my mind stirring with the sound of Vaughan Williams' music as if it were coming from everything around me that had breath. Standing in the midst of the gap in the skyline of Lower Manhattan and reflecting upon the depths of inhumanity at Ground Zero. And feeling diminutive and awe-inspired amid the giant

Redwoods (*Sequoiadendron giganteum*) of the Californian Sierra Nevada.

Unlike the Sierra Nevada, in Britain we have hardly any landscape that is untouched by human hand and so can be described as truly natural. The landscapes before us are for the most part a product of human intervention and centuries of development. That might be through careful management, such as heather moorland being burned in strips to provide the young new growth, interspersed with the mature plants, to maximize red grouse (*Lagopus lagopus scotica*) populations, or through legal changes, such as the field patterns and hedgerows, or cultural changes, such as the townscapes and patterns of our larger cities. Planting, ploughing, grazing and stone-moving, in springtime and harvest, have each left their mark.

Yet this has also left a legacy of a great diversity of landscape. We can be on the rugged fells with the odd tree on the horizon, bent crooked and gnarled with the wind in its back. We descend to the patchwork of hedgerows surrounding ridge and furrow-lined fields, a low sun marking their lines in shadow as they trace out earlier agricultural ways, before we venture along the coastal cliffs, fossils protruding from the heap of rock and clay that has been brought down by the pounding action of the tides. Ours is a countryside filled with beauty, from the widest canvases of scenery to the hedgerows' spring flowers nodding in the breeze and the seeping lines cutting through a tidal salt marsh. Thankfully there are still some places in this heavily populated nation where one can encounter tranquillity and get away from it all.

The fact that I come across people who say that they don't find God in a church building but do in a landscape is both sad and exciting. Sad because our liturgy, prayers and music, the very aesthetic of our worship, often do not connect with people. Exciting because it allows us to ask questions and to explore new avenues. How can some of the challenge, continuity and community found within formal liturgy be taken out into landscapes so that encountering and worshipping God within landscape might be part of our everyday life, and a continuation of ancient Christian traditions, rather than left to a New Age interest? And how can the natural world be drawn into the life of our liturgy within church buildings again? Can landscapes be a resource for faithful people overburdened by church life to rest awhile away from all the baggage that comes with praying in their own church buildings so that they might relax, enjoy and be re-energized by and in the life of God? Could landscapes be a doorway into a new commitment and discipleship by being the venues for the God of mission's invitation? This route is one envisaged by the Bishop of Oxford, John Pritchard, who recently commented, 'the natural world could be the way back for many whose faith has faded under the assault of too much institutional religion'.[2] The fact is that landscape is already playing a part, with a national survey suggesting that between 1987 and 2000 an awareness of a sacred presence in nature increased in the British population from 16 to 29 per cent.[3] John Inge, now Bishop of Worcester, recalling the experiences of Moses, Paul and the Emperor Constantine and noting recent research about spiritual experience, concluded that 'not only have such sacramental encounters been at the heart of some of the most important developments of the Church, they are very common among ordinary people'.[4] As we wait on a God we don't fully know and will never fully understand, the natural world conveys something of the mystery and wonder of God that might just provoke the inspiration to be amazed.

This link with the landscape is already drawn into the iconography of many of our church buildings: the green men spewing their hedgerow meal from roof bosses; the carved foliage climbing many a pillar and capital; the stained-glass windows that take us to another place; the ordinary grain and fruit of the land that as bread and wine become extraordinary gifts for us to receive at the altar. It is also there in our hymnody as we sing, for example, of that awesome wonder evoked 'when through the woods and forest glades I wander and hear the birds sing sweetly in the trees; when I look down from lofty mountain grandeur, and hear the brook and feel the gentle breeze'.[5] But do we connect with this any longer?

Revelation through nature has long been treated with suspicion by the Church. We see hostility from the likes of St Anselm (1033–1109) who, according to the art historian Kenneth Clark, maintained 'that things were harmful in proportion to the number of senses which were delighted, and therefore [he] rated it dangerous to sit in a garden where there are roses to satisfy the senses of sight and smell, and songs and stories to please the ears'.[6] Some Protestant reformers were also hostile, believing that the landscape contained no trace of divine presence within it and all saving knowledge was revealed only in Scripture. Martin Luther (1483–1546) was particularly concerned and argued that claiming to discover the essential nature of God in creation would lead to a self-glorification where the individual wished to know God on their own terms.

All of this stems from a much earlier notion, of Israelite religion leaving behind nature gods and mythology, together with their previous understanding of natural places being imbued with God, in favour of following the Lord. We see an attack on nature myths and religions as a continued theme in the Old Testament. Max Oelschlaeger argued this point, commenting that there are 'lingering reverberations of the Palaeolithic mind, especially as revealed in the symbolic significance of shepherd and wilderness for the Hebrews',[7] and that 'the Hebrews desacralized nature and viewed it as the creation of a transcendent God'.[8] Magnified through the course of Judaeo-Christian history, this leads directly to today's suspicion of New Age movements, talking with plants, and hugging trees.

This book reimagines our history and sees again how finding God in landscape is part of an honourable tradition. Through the exploration of eight different landscapes, my aim is to celebrate something of the enchantment of these places. Many of them appear in the cycle of themes for the Season of Creation in the four weeks leading up to the Feast Day of St Francis of Assisi (4 October) and so this book may also be a resource for preachers and study groups during that period. Above all, I hope that it will encourage a looking at the world with fresh eyes so as to be enchanted by the wonder of God all around us.

1

The contours of landscape

There is nothing that quite prepares you for the view of Yosemite National Park in California as you approach from the south along State Route 41. You drive out of a road tunnel and laid out before you, like giant chess pieces, are the polished granite peaks of El Capitan and Half Dome lined up in the massive glacier-carved valley. Cascading down the valley side is the Bridalveil Fall with its mist cloud underskirt and the metronome thud of water onto rock. The valley floor is lined with trees, each looking matchstick frail but collectively giving a green haze. The viewpoint is busy, even frenetic. I joined a crowd of people each keen to have a photograph taken of themselves in front of this magnificent view, all the while seeing everything around them through the screen of a digital camera. There was much polite jostling for position. Two war-wounded and dishevelled sparrows adventurously moved among the people, searching for crumbs dropped from sandwiches being eaten, while tour guides yelled out that their charges needed to be back on the bus in five minutes. I found myself wanting to yell as well. Perhaps deep down it was because I wanted to see if this valley had an echo; to fill it for a moment with my own presence. Instead I kidded myself that it was because I wanted a different experience from the one that I was having. I wanted to ask those around me just to stop, to listen, to look, to join me in taking in this scenery slowly.

This view was saved from exploitation and destruction, and the right legal safeguards put in place to allow future generations to enjoy the incredible landscape, by the Scottish émigré John Muir (1838–1914). Relatively unknown in the land of his birth, he is praised in the United States as one of the greatest prophets of conservation. While schooled in Christianity, the impact of the landscape meant that he began to see what was around him in new ways. It was as if he could now read sermons in the lines marked on stones, his choirs were the crashing sounds of waterfalls, and he felt the sacred in what he described frequently as the great temple of Nature. He 'thought of the natural world as pure and good, rather than depraved and dangerous as had many Protestants in earlier eras'.[1] Muir never became an atheist but, Max Oelschlaeger argued, 'he simply outgrew the constrictions of conventional faith and developed a theology of the wilderness' which was 'rooted in the consciousness of the sacrality of wild nature'.[2] Denis Williams commented that this was because Muir began to see another 'primary source for understanding God: the Book of Nature'.[3]

Much of his philosophical world-view, of a sense of encountering the divine in the landscape, was formed when he was in his late twenties, while walking from Indiana to Florida. This was a distance of nearly 1,000 miles. On 20 March 1870, Muir wrote to his brother David:

I am sitting here in a little shanty made of sugar pine shingles this Sabbath evening. I have not been at church a single time since leaving home. Yet this glorious valley might well be called a church, for every lover of the great Creator who comes within the broad overwhelming influences of the place fails not to worship as he never did before. The glory of the Lord is upon all his works; it is written plainly upon all the fields of every clime, and upon every sky, but here in this place of surpassing glory the Lord has written in capitals.[4]

For most of his life, Muir held a panentheistic world-view, though his later writing has a strong leaning towards pantheism. Pantheism, coming from the Greek for 'all-God', sees nature and God as being identical. Panentheism, from the Greek for 'all-in-God', sees God 'suffused throughout his creation but never reduced to identify with it'.[5] Put simply, pantheism sees that God is the whole, whereas in panentheism, the whole is in God.

While Muir balanced a dichotomy in his philosophy between civilization and nature, with nature as superior, this was underpinned by a God active in creation. As such Muir saw that we can learn from nature and be restored to our true selves when we strip away our layers of self-protection and immerse ourselves in it. He wrote, 'Everybody needs beauty as well as bread, places to play in and pray in, where Nature may heal and cheer and give strength to body and soul alike.'[6]

Overlapping some of Muir's life was the British historian G. M. Trevelyan (1876–1962), who was greatly influential in the National Trust's acquisition of historic landscapes and in later life was Master of Trinity College, Cambridge. While he was averse to Christianity, being a somewhat aggressive agnostic, he borrowed from the faith's sacramental tradition, describing the then modern passion for mountains, rocks and moors as 'one of the sacraments prepared for man or discovered by man'. He saw the value of rural landscapes for the welfare of, and remedy to, his perception of the ills of urban people. As such he regarded the landscape as being deeply ingrained in the concept of Englishness. In *Must England's Beauty Perish?*, written in 1929, he set out the goals and work of the National Trust. He was fearful that the Trust might not achieve its goals, that the 'happiness, souls, and health' of the English people 'would be in danger' and that 'without vision the people perish, and without natural beauty the English people will perish in the spiritual sense'.[7] Many who don't regularly attend church, but encounter God in landscape, would agree with this sentiment.

But what is landscape? It's something that is physical, can be touched, moved around within, observed and explored; as such it is out there in a real way, not just as a picture. How we look at landscapes can lead to a series of tensions. At times we may look from a distance, at others it is as if we have zoomed in to look deep within our sight. So the closeness or distance between the observer and the observed changes the perspective. Another dynamic, which has clear parallels with the Christian understanding of God's immanence and transcendence, is around whether we are detached and observing, noting details as if looking at a painting in an art gallery, or part of the scene as a participant dwelling within the landscape, moving around inside it and knowing it with a degree of intimacy. Are we present and in relation to everything that is happening, or distinct and removed?

Simon Schama reminded us, in his monumental work *Landscape and Memory*, that 'landscape is a work of the mind. Its scenery is built up as much from strata of memory as from layers of rock.'[8] So another tension lies between how we have been conditioned to view scenery from a particular perspective, and the actual physical piece of land that can be mapped and described in front of us. These pieces of land are also read through the story of our culture and are not just the work of nature. As was mentioned in the Introduction, there are very few landscapes in Britain that have escaped cultural changes and can, in any sense, be described as natural: perhaps just a few cliff ledges that have only been manipulated by climate changes or atmospheric pollution. These cultural changes were famously charted by W. G. Hoskins in his classic 1955 book *The Making of the English Landscape*,[9] and its contemporary equivalent, written by Francis Pryor, *The Making of the British Landscape*.[10]

In John Muir's writings we can see some of these tensions. He lived within his landscape, dwelt in it, delighted in the nature and the cultural story of the place, but then needed to withdraw from it so that he could see things from a distance – so crucial for lobbying policy-makers. By immersing himself in the landscape of the High Sierra, his writings reveal something of the divine beauty of that place. But do we have the eyes to see, the ears to hear, the imagination to connect with the landscapes around us? Often we don't. One day the Welsh poet R. S. Thomas (1913–2000) saw, and ignored, the sun glimmering on a field that he was walking by. Later, in the poem, 'The Bright Field', he lamented his lack of attentiveness to the gift of that moment:

> I have seen the sun break through
> to illuminate a small field
> for a while, and gone my way
> and forgotten it. But that was the pearl
> of great price, the one field that had
> the treasure in it. I realize now
> that I must give all I have
> to possess it. Life is not hurrying
>
> on to receding future, nor hankering after
> an imagined past. It is the turning
> aside like Moses to the miracle
> of the lit bush, to a brightness
> that seemed as transitory as your youth
> once, but is the eternity that awaits you.[11]

So how do we make those connections between the Christian faith and the contours of landscape? St Paul wrote to the Romans, 'Ever since the creation of the world his eternal power and divine nature, invisible though they are, have been understood and seen through the things he has made' (Rom. 1.20). His understanding was a continuation of the psalmist's poetry that declared, 'the heavens are telling the glory of God; and the firmament proclaims his handiwork' (Ps. 19.1). If we begin with the premise that God is omnipresent, equally everywhere or nowhere, then God is encountered both in places of startling beauty as well as in those places of ugliness that we find challenging and that ask of us, 'Where is God here?' Jeremiah noted God's self-description, 'Am I a God near by, says the LORD, and not a God far off? Who can hide in secret places so that I cannot see them? says the LORD. Do I not fill heaven and earth? says the LORD' (Jer. 23.23–24). God is therefore as present in the wonder of beauty as in the human disasters that we create and the landscapes of natural disasters, among them earthquake, fire, flood, tsunami and storm, that we suffer. In the former part we are reminded of the first creation story where each day God reviews what has happened and notes, in satisfaction, 'it was good'. Howard Jacobson described this, in his Man Booker prize-winning *The Finkler Question*, as, 'Good meaning more than good – good meaning congruent, perfected, harmonious. Good as an expression of the absolute rightness of the universe.'[12] In the latter part, where that beauty is disfigured by human action or natural disaster, there is a yearning for restoration, so that again that place might reflect the beauty of God in all its glory.

But what is beauty? Beauty is an expression of, and comes from, God's very beautiful self. It is not simply something that is in the eye or mind of the beholder. Rather it is a sacred manifestation of God's immanent power in nature, whereby 'beautiful forms may not be the "fingers" of God in creation, but they certainly can be seen as the "fingerprints" of God'.[13] Gerard Manley Hopkins (1844–89), the Jesuit poet, was clear about this. In his poem 'The Leaden Echo and the Golden Echo', he wrote: 'Give beauty back, beauty, beauty, beauty, back to God, beauty's self and beauty's giver'.[14] Its appreciation is, therefore, a gift that enables us to see more into the mystery of God, taking one outside of the self. Where this can become skewed is in the worship of beauty for itself; rather than beauty being a gateway to the transcendent, it becomes in itself idolatrous.

It is one thing to observe beauty and be thankful, but there is also a sense of entering into that beauty more profoundly. C. S. Lewis put it this way: 'We do not want merely to see beauty . . . We want something else that can be put into words – to be united with the beauty we see, to pass into it, to receive it into ourselves, to bathe in it, to become part of it'.[15] He went on to complain that 'we have peopled air and earth and water with gods and goddesses and nymphs and elves' because we have not grasped the incarnation that draws us into God. When this is grasped, we find that all that is beautiful then points to the one who is beautiful and created it all. All beauty points back as well as forwards, something that the theologian Nicholas Berdyaev said 'is either a memory of Paradise or a prophecy of the transfigured world'.[16]

This notion was particularly developed in the writings of the twentieth-century Swiss theologian Hans Urs von Balthasar. Balthasar wrote *The Glory of the Lord*, a seven-volume work subtitled *A Theological Aesthetics*, in which he describes how the beautiful is a foundation for his theological understanding:

> Beauty is the word that shall be our first. Beauty is the last thing which the thinking intellect dares to approach, since only it dances as an uncontained splendour around the double constellation of the true and the good and their inseparable relation to one another . . . No longer loved or

fostered by religion, beauty is lifted from its face as a mask, and its absence exposes features on that face which threaten to become incomprehensible to man.[17]

For Balthasar, beauty's purpose is to connect humanity to the transcendent, and this happens when beauty is surrounded by goodness and truth, so bringing the individual to a place of awe and wonder. All that the observer can then do, in the face of God's utter transcendence, is simply to worship. This is seen, with his usual enthusiasm, in the opening lines of Gerard Manley Hopkins' poem of thanksgiving, 'Pied Beauty' (1877):

> Glory be to God for dappled things –
> for skies of couple-colour as a brinded cow;
> for rose-moles all in stipple upon trout that swim;
> fresh-firecoal chestnut-falls; finches' wings;
> landscape plotted and pieced – fold, fallow, and
> plough;
> and áll trádes, their gear and tackle and trim.[18]

Among the documents of the Second Vatican Council there was a recognition that God discloses himself in what is beautiful in creation: 'God, who creates and conserves all things by His Word, provides constant evidence of Himself in created realities.'[19] For a Protestant understanding of aesthetics, Jonathan Edwards (1703–58), theologian and missionary to the Native American people, is worth exploring. Much of his theological interest lay in the concept of beauty: seeing the laws of nature being derived from God. He saw God as being beautiful, with a secondary beauty (because it is not perfect) in all creation: 'All the beauty to be found throughout the whole creation is but the reflection of . . . the diffused beams of that Being who hath an infinite fullness of brightness and glory.'[20] This world was, to Edwards, saturated with beauty in the 'harmony of sounds, and the beauties of nature', though this was only truly discernible by 'the saints' (the elect).

8

T. S. Eliot, in his poem 'Burnt Norton', which forms part of the *Four Quartets*, uses the phrase 'still point of the turning world'[21] to describe landscapes where God is experienced. Christianity's fear of pantheism, stemming from its Jewish roots, has led to a distrust in seeking God in such places. David Brown argued that 'the biblical revolt against nature cults encouraged society in directions where the sense of the mystery of the world was undermined',[22] going on to suggest that 'it may be right that while the Hebrew prophets were right in their day, the Church now pays too high a price, conditioning its followers to expect only a disenchanted world'.[23] A move back towards the enchantment of landscape can be found in the Celtic tradition, with the understanding of certain landscapes being 'thin' places where somehow 'the wondrous power of the divine could be seen breaking into the world's alleged ordinariness'.[24] Philip Sheldrake commented:

> The Christian Celts were as concerned as their ancestors had been about the issue of the sacred landscape and about good or evil places. They accepted that two worlds came together at certain familiar places in the landscape. Christian ascetics therefore sought out places where, in some special way, heaven appeared to meet earth.[25]

Iona, Lindisfarne, Glastonbury and Walsingham are much-quoted examples of holy places set within a wider landscape. A study in Northumberland concluded that such sacred places were 'a place of and for cultural memory, a place where strata of meaning have been gathered and deposited', noting that 'some of these meanings may lie dormant for a while, but they are nevertheless ready, there, to be reactivated by new stories, new histories'.[26] There are also those less-frequented places, and those places that have become special within the story of our own lives, where God has appeared more transparent. This sense of stopping and being brought up short can, of course, happen anywhere. If God is God, then God is always God in every location.

Why, then, can there be this ease of encounter? I suggest that these places are about *attentiveness* in our looking and *anchorage* within our history.

Being within a landscape can alter our sense of attentiveness. Things can appear different from the normal or the ordinary. By stilling ourselves, time, which seemingly we do not have enough of and which slips so easily from our grasp, can also seem to slow down in its perpetual motion. What do we hear, taste, touch, smell and see? Even if St Anselm would have disapproved, we use all our senses to chart out the landscape and to begin to describe it. This leads to a heightened awareness, a meticulous observation of detail, and a contemplative reflection as we begin to explore the wonders beyond the material. Michael Mayne remarked:

> for a moment you feel as one with what you see or hear; they appear to transcend time as we know it (and sometimes place as well) and have a universality about them; and they leave you with a joyful sense that ultimately 'all is well'.[27]

When we first view a landscape we do so with a freshness of vision. We take the landscape seriously on its own terms. At first sight, snow in the Arctic can appear deep blue in colour, but then after time, as our conditioning takes over, it simply appears white. Similarly with grass. Of course it is green, but is it really? This careful awareness may well lead into a reflection upon God. So the crashing waves below a coastal footpath might connect us with a sense of the power of God. Standing on a mountaintop might give us a sense of the creativity of God that stretches as far as the eye can see. Sitting watching the colours of a sunset might elicit the response, 'Isn't this peaceful?' and a sense of feeling at one as we gain an insight into the stillness of God and experience the sheer joy of the moment. The American landscape theologian Belden Lane has noted:

> The long, silent contemplation of a vast, indifferent terrain has been shown, throughout human experience, to be a powerful force in subverting self-consciousness, pushing the outer edges of language, evoking the deepest desire of the human heart for untamed mystery and beauty.[28]

Henry Thoreau, the transcendental radical philosopher (1817–62), gave his rationale for being drawn into and living among the natural environment of Maine when he wrote, 'I went to the woods because I wished to live deliberately . . . I wanted to live deep and suck out the marrow of life.'[29] He also said:

> we need the tonic of wilderness . . . At the same time that we are earnest to explore and learn all things, we require that all things be mysterious and unexplorable, that land and sea be infinitely wild, unsurveyed, and unfathomed by us because unfathomable.[30]

Beauty, wonder and simplicity, in other words enchantment, can all be evoked as we see the extraordinary in the ordinary. But the landscape can also frighten us, making us feel small, impotent and insignificant, as we cower in awesome wonder, before it, and thus before God.

So to my second point, about landscapes being anchorage in our history.

Our senses, and what we encounter, might well link us to an earlier part of our life story. Landscapes provide anchor points in a changing world, drawing us back to earlier experiences, good and bad, 'because the experience is linked with memory traces of the experience of childhood, that time when we observe each object with a pristine sense of delight,' noted Michael Mayne.[31] I know that if I have trouble sleeping I can start to replay in my mind a walk made nearly 20 years ago. Reimagining the smell of the heather, the views, the steepness of the valley, the warmth of the sun, the scurrying clouds as if in fast motion overhead, must relax me (or bore me) sufficiently for sleep, because I never seem to get to the end of the walk! Walter Brueggemann describes this sense of anchorage as having historical meaning because of the memory of an interaction:

> Place is . . . where some things have happened that are now remembered and that provide continuity and identity across generations. Place is space in which important words have been spoken that have established identity, defined vocation, and envisioned destiny. Place is space in which vows have been exchanged, promises have been made, and demands have been issued.[32]

Landscapes also resonate with stories that are steeped in our culture, national consciousness and identity. We speak of 'knowing one's place', though occasionally having to 'put someone in their place' if something has been 'put out of place' while one has been 'going places'. Simon Schama, in *Landscape and Memory*, talked of landscapes being places of memory and charted this in connection with forests, water and mountains. He commented that:

> if the entire history of landscape is indeed just a mindless race towards a machine-driven universe, uncomplicated by myth, metaphor and allegory, where measurement not memory is the absolute arbiter of value, then we are indeed trapped in the engine of our self-destruction.[33]

Instead we bring our own associations and connections, 'many of the feelings and perceptions with which our culture and our history have equipped us', as John Habgood remarked,[34] even if we have not previously seen that particular landscape in our gaze. Thus our experience is always linked with story, and the revelation gets bound up in the individual's, and the community's, ongoing narrative.

In literature, including religious stories, we encounter the myths of inaccessible peaks, unexplored rivers, lost islands and imaginary deserts, all of which people have longed to discover and add to the map of the 'known' world. This fuelled the enthusiasm and bravery of explorers. Some came home with nothing to add other than further myths. Others turned myth into reality, such as the six British explorers, including Alfred Wallace (1823–1913) and Henry Bates (1825–92), who explored, catalogued, and sent specimens home to England, of the natural history of the mythical massive river flowing east in South America. A plaque in the Anglican cathedral of the Diocese of the Amazon in Belém records the Amazon river explorers of 1848, who 'exemplify the noble tradition and lofty ideals of our race and whose lives and achievements are an inspiration to all who follow'.

Their enthusiasm for discovery and their enjoyment of new landscapes is very much a product of the Romantic movement of the late eighteenth and early nineteenth centuries. Prior to this, landscapes, and particularly mountains, were seen as hostile and fearful. Countryside was regarded as a place of toil, though also as the playground of the rich. As David Dimbleby commented, 'it was believed that truly civilised life was only possible in towns', and:

> It took the vision of artists and writers, particularly over the last three hundred years, to lead people towards an understanding of [the countryside's] natural beauty, to see things that they had never looked at, and so come to realise that the British landscape was to be cherished.[35]

Thus, take, for example, the landscape of the Scottish Highlands, which we can read in numerous theological ways.

These include: the grandeur and wonder of a creator God; a resource given to us by God to harvest, mine and use for our own benefit; a place for us to protect biodiversity as God's good stewards; an area that speaks of injustice following the Highland Clearances in the eighteenth and nineteenth centuries, where many thousands of Highlanders were forced off their land and sent to the Lowlands or abroad to make way for more profitable sheep farming; a place of human enjoyment, delight and recreation for walkers, skiers and mountain bikers; an area ripe for human flourishing through economic development and renewal. There are other views, many of which are contested as they are not mutually complementary.

Indeed, the way we look at the Scottish landscape has been moulded by the influence of art. The ideal tourist vista frames a view of mountains in the background, a loch and ruined castle in the middle ground, and cattle, or ideally a stag with multi-pointed antlers, up close. We call that 'a fine view' and the tour buses roll from one roadside lay-by to another, disgorging passengers with cameras at the ready. Such a pastoral view became highly popular in the Romantic period, reaching its apogee with the patronage of Queen Victoria during her Highland travels and the building of her cultured Scottish landed vision on the banks of the River Dee at Balmoral. Queen's View, looking down Loch Tummel with the peak of Schiehallion in the distance, still carries her name. These views resonate through the work of Edwin Landseer (1802–73), whose *Monarch of the Glen* (1851), originally painted for the House of Lords, enshrines 'the type of thrilling wildness and noble beauty that drew people to the Highlands throughout the nineteenth century and beyond',[36] and Horatio McCulloch (1805–67), particularly in the rugged grandeur of *My Heart's in the Highlands* (1860). They speak of the majesty of God in creation. Yet look more closely at the art of the same period and you also find examples that speak of God in other ways. Thomas Faed (1826–1900) painted a moving scene in *Last of the Clan* (1865), depicting a frail elderly clansman, slumped on a pony (it too looking equally miserable and downcast), ready to say farewell to his family and friends as they prepare to board a ship that will take them to another continent as part of the forced emigration of the 1840s. It is unlikely that they will ever meet again. This painting quietly protests at the injustice of it all.

We see a celebration of the diversity of the Scottish landscape in the work of the contemporary artist John Lowrie Morrison (1948–). Signing himself 'Jolomo', his paintings are celebrations of the glory of the natural landscape, conveying in equal measure both the transcendence and immanence of God, through the play of light and the intimacy of many of the images: the motif of the croft, a peat stack, washing on a line, a swinging gate, a boat drawn up on the shore. Serving as a Reader in the Church of Scotland, he connects the vibrant colours that he uses with his religious faith, giving them symbolic meaning. Linking to Renaissance ideas of colour being representational, with red being the colour of the glory of God, and blue for purity, Brian Blench, former Keeper of Decorative Arts at Glasgow's Kelvingrove Art Gallery and Museum, says that Jolomo's

> use of colour carries a parallel programme of emotions: red conveys excitement, orange is warming and energising, yellow stimulates confidence and draws the eye. In many of his paintings, blue is frequently a key colour used for its calming and healing properties, while the associated violets and indigos stimulate awareness and intuition respectively.[37]

He goes on to talk about how a Jolomo canvas will frequently contain a high key colour, balanced with a darker pigment – an almost chiaroscuro effect, though not in a late-Renaissance way merely for dramatic visual effect. For him it serves as an allegory of the struggle of the human spirit – a constant battle between light and darkness.

In such a way Jolomo is both carefully looking at the landscape and conveying something of its historical and contemporary meaning through capturing the marks that humanity has made upon it. His work, with its current popularity, is influencing a new generation and seeping into their memory of how to read a landscape.

Through attentiveness and anchorage, in this moment of personal connection with God within a landscape, so we receive God's gift of grace; the active work of God drawing us out to be the people that we truly are in him. This view was supported by David Brown, in his book *God and Enchantment of Place*:

> The excitement of place, as with the natural world, is of a God valuing more than the simply human, and instead using the material, even where decisively shaped by human beings, to tell us something of himself and thereby draw us more deeply into his presence.[38]

In a 2005 study, 30 Tasmanian respondents were asked to describe the spiritual values of wilderness; two-fifths of those questioned mentioned peace, tranquillity, serenity, harmony, and relaxing as being important, closely followed by one-third who mentioned connection, interconnectedness, and oneness with both human and non-human life forms.[39] Landscapes thus have the capacity to reveal a world and self beyond our knowing. They become sacramental. There is an in-breaking towards God's presence as God makes himself known through the whole created order. This is not at our beckoning, but is God's freely given gift. God chooses to reveal Godself. John Habgood described sacramentalism as 'perceiving a deeper meaning in things through the transforming presence of Christ',[40] and, influenced by the work of the Orthodox theologian Alexander Schmemann, concluded that it offers the possibility of living in the world with everything in it as the revelation of God. For Schmemann, 'God blesses everything he creates, and, in biblical language, this means that he makes all creation the sign and means of his presence and wisdom, love and revelation', so that: 'All that exists is God's gift to man, and it all exists to make God known to man, to make man's life communion with God.'[41]

It does, however, need to be remembered that this is not some general revelation, but is experienced in a particular place and in a particular way. Neither does God turn up on demand; the encounter cannot be forced because the initiative always lies with God and God shows himself in often the most unexpected of ways. Nor does the place in itself have meaning: 'it is the experience of place which gives meaning to place, not the attributes of place which are able of themselves to occasion meaning'.[42] It is what we bring to our view that makes the landscape have a spiritual quality – nature is not holy on its own. Nor is the theophany some special private moment, though it may be experienced alone, because it is part of that love, which continually pours forth from God, drawing the whole creation into a unity of renewal and its ultimate fulfilment in God's self. John Habgood argues persuasively that 'to perceive God's graciousness in nature is to see the world in a new light, and to bring to it a new degree of penitence and hopefulness'.[43] There is, rightly, a lament that landscapes, habitats and species have been lost for ever because of humanity's power of destruction. Equally, much work has been completed around the emergence of a Christian ecological theology that sees the need for a right stewardship of all of creation. This is particularly seen when humanity walks, in every way, more gently on the earth.

Our encounter with landscapes, as seen earlier, leads to experiences of God both transcending landscape and immanent within it. What these metaphors do is help our struggling articulation of experience whereby transcendence attempts to speak of God being other and distant and non-physical, and immanence speaks about something of God's close presence and engagement. While this is valuable, it must not polarize our thinking. David Brown warns against such polarization:

> the danger in heeding only the transcendence is that an unbridgeable gap is created between ourselves and God; the danger in accepting only immanence is that the divine is reduced to something like ourselves, his reality in effect treated as equivalent to the totality of the world.[44]

Our experience can move us to one or the other, but something of the Christian journey is a holding together in creative tension these two understandings of our experience of God.

Transcendence and immanence have been two characteristics of God that artists have grappled with in the emergence of their technique. Landscapes, together with birds, animals and objects, appear in European medieval art but only to convey greater meaning, through symbolism, placed around the human subject. They catalogue the subject within their cultural and physical place. What emerged during the seventeenth century was an attempt to allow landscape to become the focus of the gaze. This was first done by letting the picture tell a wider biblical or mythological story. The French artist Nicolas Poussin (1594–1665) was an important developer of this style, with landscape forming a graceful background in his works, even overshadowing figures, such as in his *Landscape with St John on Patmos* (1640) and *Landscape with a Roman Road* (1648). We also see examples of this style in the paintings of Claude Lorrain (*c.*1600–82), who worked mostly in Italy in an era when landscape painting was seen as an aesthetic viewpoint that lacked moral seriousness and so commanded little patronage. However, Lorrain's paintings portrayed themes that are mythical or religious, particularly with the inclusion of temples and other buildings in his landscapes, and his pictures set the wider landscape very much within a human constructed world. If, for example, he painted the sea's horizon, it was from the viewpoint of a bustling harbour. Much later, John Constable (1776–1837) was to describe him as 'the most perfect landscape painter the world ever saw', and say that in Lorrain's landscapes 'all is lovely – all amiable – all is amenity and repose; the calm sunshine of the heart'.[45]

As landscape painting grew as a genre, the trend moved towards an authentic copying on canvas of the aesthetic qualities that artists saw before them, using the right sense of proportion and aspects of light. Some artists, however, as David Brown has commented, felt 'justified in modifying the landscape before them in order to clarify a sense of divine presence or action upon the environment',[46] and this was achieved 'in two contrasting ways. On the one hand, landscapes of immanence suggested the near presence of God within the world itself; on the other, those where transcendence was stressed invited awe at the wonder of what God had achieved in the creation.'[47]

Examples can be seen in the English Romantic work of John Constable and his great rival J. M. W. Turner (1775–1851). Constable, a High Church Anglican, painted an ordered and gentle rural world delighting in God's creation. In his painting *The Cornfield* (1826), for example, the divine is marked by the inclusion of a small church in the far distance. Turner, of all British artists of the period, captured the sublime in the landscapes that he painted. By sublime I mean the awe-inspiring, savage grandeur of the natural world unmastered by humanity. The use of light in his paintings portrayed a connection with God's spirit, and Turner experimented with the different ways that light falls on water to convey, as a forerunner to the impressionistic style, the activity of God in the world. This can be seen in *Light and Colour (Goethe's Theory) – the Morning after the Deluge – Moses Writing the Book of Genesis* (1843), a painting that looks at the great flood story of Genesis, with the passive role of man unable to control nature. The painting illustrates Turner's belief that God is in charge, creating the flood, bringing Noah to the rescue, and inspiring Moses to write the book of Genesis. For this Turner absorbed Goethe's theory of light and darkness, which states that the creation of colour is dependent on the distribution of dark and light reflecting through a transparent object and leads to an infinite amount of colour variation. Turner depicts this with immense skill.

The next stage in the development of landscape painting came from a group of artists in the United States who were influenced by Constable and Turner, calling themselves the Hudson River School. While they varied in their religious convictions, the members' concern was to portray the majesty of creation and so the transcendence of God. They achieved this by using a realistic and detailed style, often idealizing nature in its portrayal, and constructing synthesized compositions of multiple scenes of natural images. This sense of awe and wonder could certainly be seen within the American landscape and the group portrayed their society's vision of exploration, discovery and settlement within that landscape. Thus, they shared a reverence for America's natural beauty with contemporary American writers such as Henry David Thoreau and Ralph Waldo Emerson (1803–82). Among their number was the Englishman Thomas Cole (1801–48), who took a steamship up the Hudson River to up-state New York in the autumn of 1825 and encountered autumnal colours the like of which he had never seen before. Later, Frederic Church (1826–1900), John Kensett (1816–72) and Sanford Gifford (1823–80) would be leading lights of the movement. Frederic Church, who was 'always concerned with including a spiritual dimension in his works',[48] exhibited *Niagara* in 1857, attracting thousands of viewers queuing round the block. This genre of painting went to the heart of the American identity, reminding people of the vast, untamed and magnificent wilderness areas of their country, and as such contributed to the movement, led by John Muir, for the creation of National Parks.

This is by necessity a broad stroke of the brush of landscape painters, but to bring this exploration into our contemporary world I want to turn to a Northumbrian artist, M. J. Forster, whose work is contained within this book and on its cover. His view of landscape is a stripping bare to its component parts in a technique that he has termed 'Überpainting'. I was struck at first by the simplicity of his watercolours, which give just the essential elements of the landscape – the shapes, shadows, and perspective – while still being instantly recognizable. In conversation he said, 'The painting process that I go through strips out all the clutter and boils it down to what the most important elements are. It's just not possible to include everything.' This draws the viewer in so as almost to be able to enter a room and look around within the painting, its exaggerated and simplified version of the subject aiding this process. 'It's hard to convey mystery,' he commented, 'and I need to rely on the imagination of the viewer. I often refer to my paintings having a sense of time or history. Yes, they are a snapshot of the present moment as well as making the viewer think what has come about to make this landscape and how it will change in the future.' Forster uses colour contrast to emphasize the important features of the landscape, building up four different washes to establish the correct range of tones so that his work 'connects with the viewers' memory or an imagined ideal that they have and I'm helping them see what they already know is there, like they have dreamed it'. As such it conveys the spiritual dimension of the landscape in a very immediate and connectable way.

The story of how landscape art emerged, from the seventeenth century onwards, affects the way we approach our viewing of a landscape. From our first look we are already shaping and interpreting what we see and so there is that inevitable mixture of seeing what is out there and what our minds think is there. We are somewhat conditioned, not least by our exposure to and understanding of landscape art in all its forms, including within the media and the subtleties of advertising, to look for the ideal and the most beautiful. In such searching we may then fail to recognize that a landscape that does not match up to all of this might still be the locality of theophany.

As we walk the different contours of the landscape, the experience of God in our lives happens in surprising and unexpected ways. The delight that we find in discovering this, when we leave our default position of inattentiveness, was described by the Trappist monk Thomas Merton (1915–68), in his last talk to the novices of his community before moving to his hermitage in August 1968:

> We are living in a world that is absolutely transparent, and God is shining through it all the time. This is not just a fable or a nice story, it is true. And this is something we are not able to see. But if we abandon ourselves to Him and forget ourselves we see it maybe frequently; that God manifests Himself everywhere, in everything – in people and in things and in nature and in events and so forth. So that it becomes very obvious that He is everywhere, He is in everything, and we cannot be without Him.[49]

This investigation now turns to how a range of landscapes reveal something more about the wonder and beauty of God. Through attentiveness and anchorage, enchantment is experienced and that which is priceless valued again.

2

Land

In mid June, as the wheat begins to turn a lighter shade of gold, the crimson red of poppies (*Papaver* sp.) floods the fields. For some reason this often does not happen in the same field in successive years; and sometimes there seem to be bumper years when I look out over the fields of the Vale of Mowbray and see numerous hazes of reddish tinge. The heads of thousands of poppies dance in the light breeze. The land recalls memories and makes connections as I look. The words 'In Flanders fields the poppies blow' swirl around my mind before lining up in regimental form as I recall 'between the crosses, row on row, that mark our place'. As the sunlight moves across the fields I see 'in the sky, the larks, still bravely singing, fly'. This First World War poem is thought to have been written in May 1915 by John McCrae, a Canadian doctor and lieutenant colonel. He had witnessed the death of a 22-year-old friend the day before and the poem was both his tribute and his protest. I think of the annual Remembrance Sunday service, with old veterans saying to young ones, 'Why have we not learnt?', and the tribute we pay to the fallen, injured and bereaved alongside the protest at the ugliness and destruction of war.

As we look across the land we cannot help but be reminded of other memories: the ridge and furrow marks of earlier agricultural settlements; the standing stones that have marked sacred spaces; the boundaries affirmed by stone crosses high on the North York Moors; or the lone trees that once were part of extensive hedge-rowed fields. Our landscape is also affected in ways that look to the future: the debates about road and rail expansion and their routes; the sites for wind turbines; and where new housing should be developed. Leaving our mark on the landscape has been something that humans have done since the beginning of time.

Marks on the landscape such as leaves pinned together, their autumn colours carefully choreographed to form a line that leads one on a journey. Or smooth mounds of sand, spiralling into the distance along a beach, waiting for the tide to turn. Sculptured cairns with stones carefully placed, vertically and horizontally, to be markers in a field. A hole in the ground, looking as if it is some creature's burrow, marked out with overlapping oak leaves. Icicles, carefully suspended, twisting round a tree. If you're walking the land and come across any of these marks on the landscape, then you might have stumbled across the work of contemporary land artist Andy Goldsworthy.

Goldsworthy uses natural materials to create sculptures that mark the land and resonate with the history and memory of the place. His materials include leaves, flowers, icicles, leaves, mud, pine cones, snow, stone, twigs and thorns. They are then at the whim of the landscape in terms of the weather, light and wind, which all contribute to the destruction of the pieces, their decay or their being washed away. Due to the ephemeral and transient nature of his art, photography plays a crucial role in capturing the work in its different states of construction, completion and decay. For Goldsworthy, 'place is crucial to his art:

a work must fit, must draw on its environment and become part of it',[1] but he is not sentimental and his work can unsettle the viewer, he says, 'just as I find nature as a whole disturbing'. He continues:

> The landscape is often perceived as pastoral, pretty, beautiful – something to be enjoyed as a backdrop to your weekend before going back to the nitty-gritty of urban life. But anybody who works the land knows it's not like that. Nature can be harsh – difficult and brutal, as well as beautiful.[2]

Knowing the land, as any farmer will tell you, is about getting out into the place and feeling the texture of the earth in your hands and the firmness of the ground beneath your feet. Walking releases chemicals in the brain that promote pleasure, just as the motion of a pram soothes a baby. People talk about 'walking off their problems'. We have lost something of this as a society with our obsession for cleanliness and the concrete and tarmac we walk on. The loss has wider implications, lessening the spiritual reflection prompted by walking the land. Studies have shown that travelling through wild and beautiful terrain, with uninterrupted views, can invoke a sense of meaning.[3] Our ancestors certainly recognized this, with their standing stones, burial mounds and other markers placed at strategic points in the landscape, from which they mapped out the places in which they lived.

Gilbert White knew the land of his native village of Selborne like the back of his hand. White was a clergyman who had been born in the vicarage of this Hampshire village in 1720 and 73 years later was to die less than a hundred metres away in a house called The Wakes. It was a simple village with a main street, a church, a green and a couple of pubs nestling in a hollow of idyllic landscape. Above the village was a beech hanger and dotted around were other woods, water meadows, hop fields and pasture. The village and its surrounding country-side was a source of daily inspiration for this country parson. Richard Mabey, the contemporary countryside writer, described it as 'the landscape of the pastoral dream made flesh: cosseted, balanced, endurable, a condensation into a single parish of almost every type and mood of scenery to be found in lowland England'.[4] In December 1788 White's *The Natural History of Selborne* was published, detailing the flora and fauna within the bounds of his parish, including the date that the swifts arrived and how they built their nests, the species flowering in the hedgerows, and the activity of bats. At a time when others were travelling to distant places in search of new species, White was content to care for his parishioners while recording and delighting in the landscape around him. By walking or riding the earth of his home he observed in minute detail its slowly changing face, from one season to another, and the presence of God infusing all that he lived among.

Earth features in the Bible's second creation story, with its beautiful imagery of the Lord moulding Adam from earth and water, like clay in the hands of a potter (Gen. 2.7). While this is poetic language and not equivalent to scientific explanation, the story does provide insights that encourage us to ask questions. Here is a wonderful intimacy between the Lord and humanity underlying the fact that humans are of the earth and belong to the earth. The word 'human' comes from the same root as 'humus' and 'humility'. Creation would not have been possible without the earth, as it is from the component chemicals of the earth that humans come and one day will return. We are part of the cycle of life and death. A healthy soil is one in which there is also death, because this is what earthworms, microbes and all the other soil fauna live on. As the liturgy for Ash Wednesday reminds us, 'Remember that you are dust, and to dust you shall return,' and the funeral rite talks of 'ashes to ashes, dust to dust'.[5] Earth receives humanity back, dust receives dust, and so death is simply a welcoming home. Job knew this, describing how 'naked I came from my mother's womb, and naked shall I return there' (Job 1.21), referring to the womb of the earth; later he dreams about being in the earth, at home in peace and rest (Job 3.13).

Genesis recounts how when Adam and Eve sinned it was the earth that was cursed, and weeds of thorns and thistles began to make it hard for humans to cultivate the soil (Gen. 3.17–18). The land suffered unjustly because of human greed in that first story of humanity's relationship with it. This place, intended for growth, went on to be violated when Cain invited Abel out to the field (Gen. 4.8–14). Instead Cain murdered Abel and his blood soaked into the earth. The blood-soaked ground cried out the injustice to God. The metaphor of landscapes crying out will be seen again in the chapters about forests and rivers where, like here, there is a linkage to contemporary groaning; the land goes on suffering from our abuse, overuse and greed. The precious topsoils are easily washed or blown away as vegetation is plundered or burned, and we find that the land is overburdened with fertilizers, pesticides and herbicides. In Madagascar, for example, the rapid rainforest clearance and extensive mining of the 1990s resulted in huge quantities of topsoil entering the river systems, so that from space astronauts could see 'Madagascar's red earth bleeding into the sea'.[6] This is a far cry from the words of the medieval mystic and horticulturalist St Hildegard of Bingen (1098–1179), who said that 'God created humankind so that humankind might cultivate the earthly and thereby create the heavenly'.[7]

The land is all that we have to keep us alive and we are utterly dependent on it. That is perhaps why the land contains our identity and our promise for the future. The vast majority of the world's population live directly off it, as small-scale peasant farmers, while many millions are officially landless. Those who are landless suffer from dislocation from their everyday needs and also the anchorage to their personal history and their collective memory. The Bible repeatedly reminds us that God is with his people in this rootless and vulnerable state, and frequently Israel is reminded that it must honour and care for its landless people. For the world's indigenous peoples the loss of their land is a cause for mourning and a sign of injustice, as having a source of food and shelter goes to the heart of human understanding and survival. If we are of the land and shaped by it, then people being denied the right of access to their land is a denial of their full humanity, as it prevents them from being attached to the earth out of whose dust they came. Their forcible removal is thus a scarring of the image of God in those likeness they are created.

This was recognized by Chief Seattle, known also as Sealth, in the nineteenth century. At a tribal assembly in 1854 he said, in response to an offer of reservation land in exchange for the land of his people, 'Every part of this earth is sacred to my people. Every pine needle, every sandy shore, every mist in the dark woods, every clearing and humming insect is holy in the memory and experience of my people.'[8] At the end of his speech he gave the conditions by which he agreed to the land exchange:

> you must teach your children that the ground beneath their feet is the ashes of your grandfathers. So that they will respect the land, tell your children that the earth is rich with the lives of our kin. This we know. The earth does not belong to man; man belongs to the earth.[9]

We see this most clearly in the way that land is treated during and after the Israelites' exodus from slavery in Egypt. During their wanderings they were a people in transit looking for the land that had been promised to them. Towards the end of the book of Deuteronomy, Moses prepares the people to enter the Promised Land. This is a land he will not set foot in; the mantle is handed to Joshua, and Moses dies in sight of the land.

But in his last days he stands in the land of Moab and offers a manifesto to define the shape and character of Israel that includes some stark alternatives between good and evil, righteousness and sin, blessing and judgement. Walter Brueggemann called this Israel's 'long reflective pause'.[10] She paused to listen at that place between landlessness and landedness. The land they had longed for was a gift; it was covenanted land filled with all those things that were so absent in the desert wanderings. They were to go on remembering this so that they would always appreciate the gift:

> Land is history with Yahweh. It is never contextless space. It is always a place where memories of slavery and manna are recalled and where hopes of fidelity and well-being are articulated. Land is always where Israel must come to terms with the Lord of memories and hopes.[11]

Much of the Old Testament is about this land of God's revelation being won and lost. Brueggemann traced the Israelites' understanding of land through different periods of their history. He illustrated that in the first 11 chapters of Genesis we see how successive people rooted in the land move towards expulsion and loss of the land. Adam and Eve (Gen. 3.14–19), Cain and Abel (Gen. 4.12), the people at the time of Noah, and the people of Babel (Gen. 11.1–9) do all they can through carelessness, deceit and error to lose their land. With the stories of Abraham, Isaac and Jacob we see a change. They were sojourners who were trusting God in a pilgrimage of faith towards a future promise of land being theirs. God made Abraham a simple promise, 'To your descendants I give this land' (Gen. 15.18), that contradicted history up to that point. Rather than Adam and Eve's expulsion and curse, now there was inclusion and promise. Rather than Cain's punishment of being driven off the soil, now there was forgiving love. Rather than destruction and sweeping away, now there was building up and a future, and rather than the scattering that followed Babel, now there was a gathering to a land. The Torah, the law, is the way that Israel can fully enjoy the gift of land; and at its heart Sabbath rest, 'a voice of gift in a frantic coercive self-serving world',[12] reminds us of this giftedness and attempts to stop our grasping temptation to try to turn the land into a non-stop machine. Whenever this was ignored, and the land was not cared for properly, the land of promise became a problem. Israel is 'always on the move from land to landlessness, from landlessness to land, from life to death, from death to life'.[13]

Of the parables of Jesus, the one that gives most focus to the land is the Parable of the Sower (Matt. 13.3–9, 18–23; Mark 4.1–9, 14–20; Luke 8.5–15), which comments on the variety of ways in which humanity receives, dismisses or simply does not hear the message of God. Jesus was using clear motifs from the rural landscape of Galilee in this parable and his hearers would have known immediately what he was describing. Small strips of terraced land, cultivated by farmers, lined the hillsides and were linked by paths edged by weeds and piles of cleared stones. His audience would have recognized the birds pecking at stray seed that landed on the paths baked hard as brick by the sun and the continual passage of people and donkey traffic. They would have known of the rocky ground at the edges of the fields where stones were thrown and how the stray seed would start off well there but then shrivel in the scorching heat as their roots were not deep enough to reach any moisture. They knew also of the impressive thistles with their long thorns and their light, wind-blown seeds that filled the soil's seed bank.

The seed grown in the cultivated soil thrives and the landscape imagined in Jesus' hearers' minds leads them to a sense of wonder as the story proceeds. Jesus, with an exaggeration that he was known for in his parables, talks about an impossibly magnificent harvest return. Jesus asks them to 'listen up', as he is about to say something amazing. Adam and Eve failed to pay attention and left with nothing, but Jesus is calling his listeners to follow in a way that leads to an extravagant abundance. Luke talks about a hundredfold increase, while Mark and Matthew settle for the lesser, though still generous, amounts of sixtyfold and thirtyfold respectively. Whichever, this landscape is one of abundance with resulting joy and thanksgiving.

Harvest festivals are times when the whole community can gather to share in this sense of joy and thanksgiving. They place a pause on our tendency to take land for granted and help us to develop a humility that values our environment and delights in the surprise of each new gift. I well remember being invited to preach at a harvest festival for a small estate village in North Yorkshire. The church was beautifully decorated and people in tweed jackets squeezed into the pews and sang all of the traditional hymns. When it came to the distribution of Holy Communion I was fascinated by people's hands. They were not the carefully manicured hands that I was used to seeing in a suburban setting, but were rough, scarred and juice-stained, with sausage-sized fingers. These were the working hands of foresters and farmers, gardeners and ghillies, joiners and jammers, and each would have a thousand tales to tell. The people had come perhaps because it was a tradition, or to be seen to be playing a part in the community, but also because of a deep need to collectively give thanks to God for another harvest safely gathered. Afterwards there was an auction of produce, and the jar of Mrs Aitken's curried apple pickle was sold, as apparently happened every year, for an amazing amount of money for charity. This typified the generous thanksgiving for the gifts that all had received.

For the Celtic peoples, as we saw in Chapter 1, thankfulness for the bounty of the land infused their prayers, especially when there was a risk that drought, flood or fire could destroy everything. For them, some landscapes more than others made it easier to offer this thanksgiving because they had more spiritual potency; such places were doorways to the sacred. Philip Sheldrake recorded that religious texts from the period speak of people 'seeking the place of their resurrection'.[14] In their 'search for holiness and spiritual experience there was a creative tension between the desire for seclusion and the wish to be accessible and open to society at large'.[15] On the small island of Oransay, a tidal island linked to Colonsay off the west coast of Scotland, there is an example of such a place. High crosses mark out the monastic enclosure as a sacred space within the landscape. As elsewhere, they are saying that this is a place where earth and heaven touch each other, and making a statement to the local community and travellers that they are crossing a border and entering a different quality of space.

The God of the Israelites was encountered in such borderlands. Belden Lane noted that, 'Yahweh frequently moves to the boundary in order to restore the centre, calling a broken people back to justice and compassion',[16] and it is in the peripheral places that identity and the community's focus are restored. Jesus also moved his disciples continually to borderlands on the landscape. These places were often outside the disciples' comfort zone, and the experience sometimes involved breaking the strict moral code of their day in order that others might have life in abundance. So we find that over the border in Tyre and Sidon, Jesus encounters a Syrophoenician woman and her daughter (Mark 7.24–30; Matt. 15.21–28), he heals a demoniac in the swine-herding country of the Gerasenes (Matt. 8.28–34; Luke 8.26–39), and he feeds the multitude on the eastern, non-Jewish side of the Sea of Galilee (Mark 8.1–10). As Lane noted, 'he knows that places on the edge, those considered God-forsaken by many, are where his identity as Messiah has to be revealed'.[17] In such a way a new centre is always being imagined, drawing us to the fact that God's centre is everywhere and circumference is nowhere. These places, marked out down the centuries, become hallowed by communities, and throughout the world's faiths we find landscapes set aside because they have been regarded as being in some way sacred.

At the 1992 Rio Earth Summit, some attempt was made to outline the value and role of different ecological landscapes, including these sacred landscapes. A new term was coined: 'ecosystem services'. These are the benefits that people obtain from ecosystems and include four areas, which have been called provisioning, regulating, cultural and supporting services. Provisioning services are the products that are obtained from ecosystems such as food, fibre, fuel, genetic resources, and natural medicines. Those benefits of ecosystems that help regulate the environment include their contributions towards air quality, local and regional climate, water catchments, erosion (vegetation retains soils and prevents landslips), waste management and disease control. The third area, cultural, covers a breadth of services: these are the non-material benefits that people obtain from ecosystems through spiritual enrichment, cognitive development, reflection and inspiration (for art, folklore, national symbols, architecture), recreation and aesthetic experiences. Underpinning these three categories of services are the supporting services: those that are necessary for all the other ecosystem services. Their impacts upon people are usually indirect, or happen over a long period of time. This area includes the classics of school biology lessons and those complicated arrow charts one had to learn: soil formation and fertility, photosynthesis and oxygen production, nutrient and water cycling.

The use of the word 'services' picks up a term usually heard in economic circles, where it describes items or functions that can be marketed and traded, thus having a monetary value. There is a debate as to whether similar economic analysis can be used to quantify our ecosystems. On the one hand, there are those who would see that a persuasive economic argument will help to put the case for greater environmental protection and proactive conservation. Of course, many provisioning services already have an economic value in our shops or land sales. Likewise with regulatory services, where a range of measurement tools exist, such as the savings made from flood protection, or monetary value from paying to visit a landscape. In the United States, the business model for National Parks includes an entry fee for every car that enters. But are there some ecosystem services that simply cannot have an economic value placed upon them because they are 'beyond price'? Some economists argue that a price can be found by asking what people would pay for a particular landscape's continued existence, as a means of fleshing out what is otherwise an intrinsic value. Others would argue that this is too anthropocentric, centred on the self and 'what I can afford', and the question that needs to be asked is a theological one, around 'What worth does God see in this landscape?' Ethical aspects may then be brought into the equation, such as the need for development, the justice around the removal of indigenous peoples, or the intrinsic right of something simply existing or being there.

Among the cultural services definitions is one for the spiritual value of an ecosystem. This appears to be split between the valuing of sacred sites for indigenous cultures (which tends to be skewed towards developing countries), and that sense of the spiritual in the landscape that provides inspiration for people's lives. According to a Millennium Ecosystem Assessment report, the loss of sacred species or sacred places, when combined with social and economic changes, 'sometimes weaken[s] the spiritual benefits people obtain from ecosystems in many parts of the world', though 'under some circumstances . . . the loss of some attributes may enhance spiritual appreciation for what remains'.[18] The commitment of religious groups to sacred forests, mountains, rivers, lakes, seas and deserts can lead to a greater level of protection for these places and their surrounding landscape. Without the ongoing commitment of these communities to pass on the oral and written traditions that make up their rituals, pilgrimages, rites and worship at such sites, it will require only a couple of generations before it is lost.

But how does one put a price on sacred places? If it was by saying, 'What can I pay you for your sacred site?' the response from the hearer would be either to walk away in disgust at the insensitive disregard of a religious cultural understanding of a place, or for them to suggest an exaggerated high price with noughts being added by the second. Sacred sites cannot be moved. Neither can you create the sacred. Nor can you command God to appear. Thus, its worth is its intrinsic value. Perhaps the greatest value of the spiritual services part of the Millennium Ecosystem Assessment is to continually remind us that a value cannot be placed on many aspects of our landscape. The first step in the dis-enchantment of the land that we live and move on is attempting to place a monetary value on its wonder.

3

Forest

Leave the main road as it rushes from Aviemore to the ski slopes of the Cairngorms, or their summertime attraction of the funicular railway, and soon you get a taste of the ancient Highlands. Here in the depth of the Abernethy forest, the path soft underfoot from the slowly rotting waxy pine needles, are some ancient treasures. Their reddish bark and gnarled, flaking trunks brood protectively over smaller trees growing up underneath from the bilberry (*Vaccinium myrtillus*) and heather (*Erica* sp.) sward. These veteran Scots pine (*Pinus sylvestris*) specimens, many of them witnesses of the 1745 Jacobite rebellion, are part of the last remnant of the great Forest of Caledon. As you walk on, so the smells of the forest fill your head: the clinical sharpness of the pine resin, the dampness and whiff of fungi, the earthy smell after recent heavy rain. Down at one's feet the floor is alive. Wood ants (*Formica aquilonia*), in a hyperactive stream of collective effort, emanate like the spokes of a wheel from their pine needle mound of a nest. Wave your hand over the nest and the smell irritates your nostrils with the pungency of a thousand squirts of formic acid. Nearby the twayblade orchid (*Listera cordata*) stands sentinel like a lighthouse in the undergrowth. Then there are the rare and unique species of mammal and bird, among them the elusive pine marten (*Martes martes*), and the capercaillie (*Tetrao urogallus*), almost always shy apart from during their 'lec' mating ritual. Across the burn, with its gurgling foam of fast-flowing water, is a distant view of the Cairngorms, a purple haze of heather-clad mountain shoulder and foreboding dark corries, painted beyond the gap in the trees.

This is just a remnant of an ancient woodland. Around 80 per cent of Britain is thought to have been originally forested; when the Romans arrived this was perhaps down to 50 per cent. With the pressure for agricultural land, and then the need for wood to be sawn into planks to build battleships, and later to stoke the fires of the industrial revolution, this fell to 5 per cent at the beginning of the twentieth century. The government, concerned about maintaining a strategic supply of timber, having come perilously close to running out of pit props in the mines during the First World War, in 1919 established the Forestry Commission. Since then there has been a gradual increase in forest cover, now covering 13 per cent of Britain.

Much of this was achieved with the planting of vast tracts of land with row after row of conifers. This annoyed many, not least the great promoter of and writer about the Lake District, Alfred Wainwright:

> the transformation of Ennerdale from beautiful valley to a dense forest is now complete and is no cause of pride. Here trees are grown unnaturally and denied space and light so that the limbs wither and only a straight main stem develops. The aim is a thicket of living telegraph poles. This is battery farming, and because trees have life and dignity it has all the objections of battery farming.[1]

Taxpayers in the UK, through the management of the public forest estate by the Forestry Commission, own just over 18 per cent of the nation's trees, woods and forests; the rest are owned by private individuals, companies and charities.[2] When the Coalition government announced in 2011 its intention to fundamentally reform the ownership of the public forest estate, suggesting that vast areas could be essentially sold off through leasing and other areas managed by charities and interest groups, there was public outrage. Members of the public started sending the government 30 pence, being the cost per person per year of the public forest estate, and, probably for the first time ever, the Socialist Workers and members of the Countryside Alliance were to be seen at the same protests. Just three weeks later, following questions to the Prime Minister, the scheme was abandoned. The Secretary of State, Caroline Spelman, said to a packed House of Commons, 'If there is one clear message from this experience, it is that people cherish their forests and woodlands and the benefits they bring.'[3]

Why are trees, woods and forests so important for people?[4] It is, in part, due to the issues of attentiveness and anchorage explored in Chapter 1, and which I now look at in turn.

Robert Louis Stevenson (1850–94), the Scottish novelist and poet, wrote: 'it is not so much for its beauty that the forest makes a claim upon men's hearts, as for that subtle something, that quality of air, that emanation from old trees, that so wonderfully changes and renews a weary spirit'.[5] People speak of entering woodland landscapes to be restored, to relax, to find refreshment and solitude, even to pray. For Thomas Merton, who lived alone in the woods of central Kentucky, the silence provided by his simple home, deep within a natural landscape, was of vital importance:

> I cannot have enough of the hours of silence when nothing happens. When the clouds go by. When the trees say nothing.

When the birds sing. I am completely addicted to the realization that just being there is enough, and to add something else is to mess it all up.[6]

Within literature there is much talk of landscapes being able to take one out of the self, so leading to enhanced purpose and meaning, an awareness of interrelationships within created matter, and a sense of oneness with nature. Charles Darwin, writing in 1839 about his travels on board the *Beagle*, said:

Among the scenes which are deeply impressed on my mind . . . none exceed in sublimity the primeval forests undefaced by the hand of man; whether those of Brazil, where the powers of Life are predominant, or those of Tierra del Fuego, where Death and Decay prevail. Both are temples filled with the varies productions of the god of Nature: no one can stand in these solitudes unmoved, and not feel that there is more in man than the mere breath of his body.[7]

This links to a biblical image that uses trees planted next to water channels so that their roots receive moisture as a metaphor for abundant living and wholeness, 'leading to a righteous life'.[8] The psalmist captures the essence of a person living within the law of God as being 'like trees planted by streams of water, which yield their fruit in its season, and their leaves do not wither' (Ps. 1.3), and that they become like specimen trees, well nurtured such as those in the Temple courts, which 'flourish like the palm tree, and grow like a cedar in Lebanon' (Ps. 92.12).

There is evidence[9] that having access to trees, woods and forests raises health through enhanced fitness and a lowered pulse rate, and that people with a view of woodland from hospital wards recover more quickly from surgery than other patients, and are discharged earlier.[10] Other research[11] has found that 'spiritual' experiences in woods and forests include feelings of being at peace in the solitude, of being comfortable in that space (existential well-being), and in descriptions of altered states of awareness ('walking taller' or feeling 'really small'). This may be because woods and forests absorb sound, so there can be a greater sense of silence (depending on the volubility of immediate wildlife) and, therefore, a greater sense of tranquillity (looked at in Chapter 9). If you compare areas of open parkland and woodland of a similar size, with the same density of people within each, the woodland appears to be less populated.

In many ways, the results of all this research should not be a surprise to us, as it was from a forested landscape that humanity as a species emerged and was shaped. Perhaps there are still components of our genetic wiring that recognize this and long to be in such landscapes: an awareness of entering into a different rhythm of life and so taking 'a moment's glimpse in a constant process'[12] in a landscape where a tree's lifespan is often much longer than that of human beings. Equally, it could be about finding an opportunity for praise in an otherwise frenetic life that has squeezed out a Sabbath rest or a *kronos* pause. Was this why St Bernard of Clairvaux (1090–1153), remarked in an Epistle, 'believe me, you will find more lessons in the woods than in books. Trees and stones will teach you what you never learn from the masters'?[13]

This sense of attentiveness can lead to trees, woods and forests being places of enlightenment. Within a three-dimensional landscape comes a fourth dimension to the experience. The ancient Oxyrynchus Papyrus, commonly called the Gospel of Thomas, contains the words, 'Lift up the stone and you will find me; cleave the wood and I am there. He that wonders shall reign.'[14] We can find plenty of biblical examples of this theophany of location even though trees in the Bible are rare places of shade, refreshment and meeting. In Genesis we read how Abraham offered hospitality to strangers, and 'The Lord appeared to Abraham by the oaks of Mamre' (Gen. 18.1ff.). Under these trees, possibly terebinth trees (*Pistacia terebinthus*), there is a divine meeting with Abraham that traces out his future. God is encountered by Moses at a burning bush (Exod. 3.2–6), by the despairing Elijah who out in the wilderness falls asleep under a solitary broom tree and is woken by an angel with fresh cake and water (1 Kings 19.4–5). In the Gospels we find Zacchaeus seeking a glimpse of Jesus from up a sycamore tree (Luke 19.2–4) and Nathaniel beginning a new life away from the shadow of his fig tree (John 1.48).

People describe encountering a sense of God's presence, an accompaniment, when they are in woods. Mark Wallace, describing his local Crum Woods on the edge of suburban Philadelphia, wrote that they are a 'place where God especially dwells'. He believes that 'a place that is sacred, is a place where nature subsists in harmony with diverse ecosystems' because 'God as Spirit inhabits the biotic support systems on which all life depends, invigorating these systems with divine energy and compassion', and so 'wherever there are places left on earth where natural ecosystems are in balance with their surroundings, there is God's presence'.[15]

Trees and forests also give us anchorage. Simon Schama has explored the various myths and stories connected to woodland and how these have entered the popular imagination as places of awe and wonder as well as fear and danger.[16] Little Red Riding Hood conveys the fear of entering a woodland not knowing what is there, yet it may be down in the woods today that you find the surprise of a teddy bears' picnic or Winnie-the-Pooh in the Hundred Acre Wood! Shakespeare fills Macbeth with paranoia as Malcolm's camouflaged army approaches, so fulfilling the warning that he would never be vanquished until Birnam Wood came to Dunsinane. The popular writer Bill Bryson is part of this fearful team:

So woods are spooky ... there is something innately sinister about them, some effable thing that makes you sense an atmosphere of pregnant doom with every step and leaves you profoundly aware that you are out of your element and ought to keep your ears pricked.[17]

A number of veteran trees have gathered around them religious stories. Joseph of Arimathea is associated with the Glastonbury Thorn which attracted a cultic reverence until the Puritans chopped the first of a number of trees down in the seventeenth century. In Perthshire the Fortingall Yew is connected with a tradition that Pontius Pilate was born beneath it or visited the nearby Roman camp. Some trees live on in the collective memory of communities, having played a part in significant events. On Jubilee Day 1877 some 95 Sunday-school children squeezed themselves into the Copthorpe Oak, together with their vicar and two churchwardens, and, in a typical English way, sang the National Anthem! A cedar of Lebanon (*Cedrus libani*) in the grounds of Rufford Abbey in Nottinghamshire had its crown lopped in memory of the executed King Charles I. There is also much folklore wisdom connected with trees and woods: for example, the rhyme that forecasts summer weather, 'Oak before ash and you're in for a splash, ash before oak and you're in for a soak', or the idea of planting rowan (*Sorbus aucuparia*) to ward off evil spirits. This memory bank idea was reinforced by research carried out in Wales: it was found that for people brought up in rural areas, 'trees do signify "home", and as such comprise an integral part of their personal and community identity'.[18]

The need for sacred space, marked out and set aside as a 'home' by the individual or community, is seen in many cultures; these places are often planted with trees, which have been invested with mythical status. The native African religions of West Africa frequently have their fetish shrines among sacred groves: 'members of the community identify a specific area in the landscape as a point of contact between the invisible and the human worlds, and establish a ritualized alliance with spiritual entities that dwell there'.[19] A survey of sacred and protected forest groves in southern Ghana found that their origins were varied, some being linked to historical events, some founded on burial grounds, while others were believed to have existed since creation. Their powers also varied: some were regarded as the home of the spirits of ancestors, others as housing protective spirits, or as places of healing. The research showed that 'the most significant factors that affect people's attitudes to the groves seem to be the strength of the traditional political and spiritual leaders, the influx of immigrants, and land pressure'.[20] These factors led to a number of taboos that govern people's behaviour in and around the groves, including who can enter, what can be harvested and when, what is protected, and how sacred days, recalling historical events when the forest deity played a role, restrict activities.

Sacred woodland groves are found in many different cultures. In India these places are often rich in rare biodiversity, because local communities prohibit hunting and timber extraction so that their Hindu deities may be honoured. In Japan, where the Sugi tree (*Cryptomeria japonica*) is regarded as sacred, groves are usually part of Shinto shrines. For Christians any pilgrimage to the Holy Land involves time in the grove of olive trees in the Garden of Gethsemane, which marks the brooding waiting of Jesus' last night. Next door, the Church of All Nations recreates this atmosphere in its vaulted architecture of tangled trees in semi-darkness.

Other examples exist of forests and woodlands that have become places where memories are held and a sense of the sacred experienced. In Staffordshire the National Memorial Arboretum is the 'living and lasting memorial to commemorate and celebrate those who gave their lives in the service of their country and all who have served and those who have suffered as a result of conflict'. It sees its role as a 'unique haven of peace, contemplation and hope for the future'.[21] Elsewhere when a local landowner was killed during the horror of the Great War, his friends gathered to plant out a cruciform shape of trees. As the trees grew so the Whipsnade Tree Cathedral become a living testament to the desire for 'faith, hope and reconciliation'.[22] The friends' inspiration was to create in living form what they saw in the architecture of the nation's medieval cathedrals. It is thought that sacred groves caught the imaginations of the architects of these great buildings, so that they built and carved in stone the experience of walking among huge trees that lifted the soul to the creativity of God. This turned full circle in April 2011, when HRH Prince William married Miss Catherine Middleton in Westminster Abbey, where the nave was lined with English field maple trees (*Acer campestre*), leading to a greater sense of enchantment in that holy place.

The twin approaches of attentiveness and anchorage, outlined above, lead directly to resourcing the wider, and often secular, environmental organizations' concerns about deforestation – something that, interestingly, is mentioned in the Deuteronomic laws. These laws assert that in sieges, you are allowed to take food from trees, and wood from dead trees, in the proximity of the town your army is besieging, but not destroy living specimens (Deut. 20.19–20). Whether this happened in practice is debatable. Trees in biblical times carried high utilitarian value partly because of their scarcity. This meant that every part of a tree had the potential to be used. The seasons brought bumper crops of fruit, including oil, which was used in both the home and for religious devotion. The supplies must have been enormous, with a record of Solomon bringing the servants of Hiram 20,000 baths full of olive oil (2 Chron. 2.10). When a tree stopped producing fruit its future was doubtful, and there is an example of this in the Synoptic Gospels when Jesus notes a fruitless fig tree (Matt. 21.19–21; Mark 11.13–14; Luke 13.6–7). These trees would then be used for fuel, with the better wood being used in construction (1 Kings 6.33–44). The best olive wood was favoured for ornate carving, including within Solomon's Temple, where it was used for the golden winged cherubim in the sanctuary and for the door posts, which were carved with palm trees, flowers and more angels (1 Kings 6.23, 31–32).

For the people of Maria Ribeira, near Gurupá on the bank of the river Amazon, who are all descendants of former slaves, the forest provides for their everyday needs. It is 'the mother that gives the quality of life and the good air we breathe', they noted during a community meeting in July 2011, and 'it is where the people here can find materials to build their houses and boats, and the food we eat'. One member of the community commented, 'I believe God is in the forest first in the air, second in the biodiversity of what God has provided in the different fruits here. Only the one above could give this diversity.'

When trees are threatened with being cut down, particularly those seen as community or historical assets, there is likely to be a public outcry, and if the destruction takes place there is a sense of community mourning. An example of this is in the West Bank where olive trees (*Olea europaea*) are a crucial part of the economy. With their branches seen by the Abrahamic faiths as symbols of peace, the destruction of so many trees during the building of the Israeli government's partition wall exacerbated the Palestinian people's sense of outrage. Culturally the tree is seen as a symbol of the longevity of a community, giving it a sense of rootedness and durability, going deep within the Palestinian sense of identity. The olive harvest is seen as a joyous family and community time, but restrictions imposed by the security zones around Israeli settlements and their access roads, together with the barrier of the partition wall, mean that some farmers can no longer reach their trees. Others have seen their ancient trees uprooted as casualties of war. Farmers are therefore stuck between a rock and a hard place. Either they leave their crops to rot or they risk their lives trying to harvest it. A *Guardian* newspaper journalist described Ahmed Kasem, a Palestinian olive farmer living a few miles south of Nablus on the Israeli-occupied West Bank. He 'enjoys curling up for a nap in the shade of one of his trees. When he is not dozing, he wanders around the olive groves, as he has done for most of his 76 years, watering the trees or tucking a little more earth round their roots to protect them from the sun.' Some of his trees were bulldozed by the Israelis, these having been planted by his grandfather 100 years before. Ahmed Kasem said, 'being with the trees is like being in heaven. I am not crazy but I open my heart to the trees. I think of the trees as I do of my family. I speak to them when I have troubles.'[23]

Across the globe, a USPG-sponsored mission partner, Ruth de Barros, has been a Christian voice campaigning against the illegal destruction of the Amazonian rainforest. Working with others, she is involved in trying to equip local people with the power to hold back the loggers. While recognizing the need for sustainable development, she has noted the negative effect that forest destruction has had on the lives and well-being of local people. There have been periodic phases of direct action, with tree dwellers and huggers campaigning against development by chaining themselves to trunks or living within the canopy. Those whose voices of protest have become too loud have been threatened, and even killed: in May 2011 two activists, José Cláudio Ribeiro da Silva and his wife Mario do Espírito Santo, were found murdered. According to Ruth de Barros, these deaths were just two of 800 people murdered while seeking to protect the rainforest, over a period of 30 years. The Anglican Church community in the locality is not silent, and takes part in 'demonstrations against those who illegally exploit the Amazon and who kill to get their way'.[24] 'The illegal companies have more power, more money, more weapons and all too often go unpunished,' de Barros wrote; 'most of the criminals go unpunished, and those who should help are often deeply involved in crime themselves as they accept bribes and benefits from the illegal companies.'[25] Sister Rebecca Squires, from the Roman Catholic Sisters of Notre Dame de Namur, has worked in Brazil for three decades ministering alongside indigenous people. She told me that in the folklore of the Guarani Indian community, their deceased grow up as trees in the forest, and so they are reluctant to cut trees down. When they do, they have a respect that entails an explanation of their need and an apology to the tree for having to cut it down. Those tribal members who are Christians see no difficulty in synchronizing this world-view with a biblical respect for the whole of creation.

All of this work draws on the Christian tradition of valuing creation and seeking justice for the voiceless. It also looks beyond the local, because the trees that are in need of protection are 'not just individual entities of ethical, aesthetic, or spiritual note, but symbols of wider nature and the landscape',[26] which is continually under threat of exploitation. Some people, though not nearly enough, are waking up to the value of these places for the quality of life. A study in Western Australia found that, while there had been a decline in religious affiliation over a period of 30 years, there had been a marked increase in respect for the spiritual value of native forests, corresponding to a greater public protest about the over-exploitation going on within them.[27] St Thomas Aquinas (*c.*1225–74), in his teaching about creation, saw that every creature, in its own unique way, has the ability to reflect the goodness of God.

> God cannot express himself fully in any one creature: and so he has produced many and diverse life forms, so that what one lacks in its expression of divine goodness may be compensated for by others: for goodness, which in God is single and undifferentiated, in creatures is refracted into a myriad hues of being.[28]

From this, I suggest that the destruction of ecosystems is both a loss in their intrinsic value and a loss to humanity of the species that live within them. More importantly, this is a loss to us also of something that gives us a mirror into God's very self.

In response to this threat, some have suggested that Martin Buber's concept of I-Thou[29] might provide a useful way to engage with trees. This involves an understanding of trees as responsive subjects and possessing agency, thus creating an interaction with us and with God. There is much in the biblical metaphorical language about trees to commend this approach. Isaiah spoke of the trees clapping their hands with joy (Isa. 55.12) and the terror of a stand of trees facing a strong wind (Isa. 7.2). Ezekiel states, in God's voice, that 'all the trees of the field shall know that I am the LORD. I bring low the high tree, I make high the low tree; I dry up the green tree and make the dry tree flourish' (Ezek. 17.24). Thus,

> to say that trees praise, sing, clap, and rejoice is to say that trees, as trees, in their whole physical, chemical, spatial, biotic functioning can fully respond to their Creator when that functioning is uninhibited and free. To say that trees groan is to say that trees experience and respond to conditions of human abuse or neglect that inhabits and closes down their responsiveness. In this way metaphors of praising and groaning enable us to 'hear' what the trees have to 'say'.[30]

The sound of wind changes as it blows through different tree species, giving them a range of 'voices'. John Muir was no stranger to this when he wrote, 'I could distinctly hear the varying tones of individual trees – Spruce and Fir, and Pine, and leafless Oak. Each was expressing itself in its own way – singing its own song, and making its own particular gestures.'[31] He famously tied himself to the top of a Douglas fir (*Pseudotsuga macrocarpa*) tree during a storm, swaying to and fro as it violently swung and creaked in the fearsome wind! Perhaps we are being invited to hear the lament and to respond to the groaning in ways that actively work to bring relief and soothe the cry. Only then might the subtlety of the sound change to be one filled with the trees clapping their hands to the praise of creation.

We see the tree repeatedly appear throughout the biblical narrative. We look back with some nostalgia to the Tree of Life in Genesis that offered the provision of life for Adam and Eve (Gen. 2.9). In medieval art it is depicted with its roots firmly in the earth and its canopy in the heavens. So also was the Tree of the Cross, described by the Welsh poet R. S. Thomas, in 'Tell Us', as God giving of himself 'on a hewn tree, suffering injustice, pardoning it, pointing as though in either direction'.[32] From this hewn tree, amid all of its degradation and inhumanity, came new hope and expectation. The link between heaven and earth, broken by Adam's sinfulness, was restored. Tradition holds that the wood for the Tree of the Cross came from the Tree of Life and, in medieval art, the moment of restoration is represented by the Tree of the Cross bursting into blossom on the day of resurrection. The iconography helps us to reconnect following our own environmental sins, and so provides a metaphor of trees being part of the ongoing salvation of the earth. This image of the involvement of trees in restoration is among the visions of John the Divine, who was exiled on the Isle of Patmos by the Roman Caesar Domitian. While there, John experienced a tour of the heavenly realms. Hope burst forth from this man who was essentially a political prisoner, and he saw trees as a symbol of God's benevolence, bringing a fruit in each season and leaves that will be the medicine of healing for the nations (Rev. 22.1–2). With some degree of foresight, John Evelyn (1620–1706), in a lecture to the Royal Society in 1662, spoke about the 'sacredness and use of standing groves', commenting that 'trees and woods have twice saved the whole world; first by the Ark, then by the Cross; making full amends for the evil fruit of the tree of Paradise, by that which was borne of the tree in Golgotha', and arguing that 'all intelligent persons have embraced the solace of shady arbours and all devout persons found how naturally they dispose our spirits to religious contemplations'.[33]

Like other landscapes, trees, woods and forests draw humanity to see and experience the gift of the divine in the ordinary. In biblical times they were places of theophany. They continue today to be landscapes where people feel open, or are opened, to the revelation of God. I imagine and hope that I see the wonder of God as light streams through the canopy, hear God's whisper in wind among the pine needles, and experience the joy of God's gift of life as I kick orange and red autumn leaves, my lungs filled with the oxygen that they have produced.

4

River

If you were brought up, as I was, on Arthur Ransome's adventures with the Swallows and the Amazons in and around the shores of Coniston Water in the Lake District, then those stories may well live in that place in your mind where fiction and fact can seem blurred. Having read some of these stories to my own children, one of our summer holidays had to be spent, in part, sailing on Coniston. I don't really know if it was for their benefit or mine!

An added bonus during that holiday was finding a book that gave suggested walks to places that are thought to have been part of the landscape of Ransome's stories. It's a kind of location guide. We know from the book *Swallowdale* that Trout Tarn is 'nearly a mile beyond Swallowdale, high on the top of the moor, a little lake lying in a hollow of rock and heather. When the Swallows saw it, they wished almost that they had made their camp on its rocky shores.'[1] A beck flows from Trout Tarn, down one waterfall into the idyllic campsite called Swallowdale, down another waterfall and eventually through steep woodland down to the southern end of the lake. The guidebook's suggested site of Swallowdale was very disappointing: a flat area of rushes and bog where no one would wish to pitch a tent. However, Trout Tarn, in reality Beacon Tarn, was a great discovery: bright blue under an August sky, with heather still meeting the water's edge along a rocky shore.

Our immediate reaction was to go swimming in this peaty water. If I kept my body floating as much as possible, within a few inches of the surface, then it felt quite warm. But allow a leg to drop down into the dark depths of the cold water and there was that immediate quickening of breath and the tightening of the stomach muscles. There in the water one felt graceful, weightless even, as from the water's surface the Lakeland peaks peeped up dark in the distance.

Water surrounds us. It makes up about 70 per cent of our bodies. During that knitting time in our mother's womb, as the psalmist (Ps. 139.13) describes it, we are enveloped in water, and the 'breaking of the waters' can often be the first sign that labour is beginning. Water is an essential part of our survival; without any to drink one would die within days. Streams, lakes and rivers provide a lifeline for food, drinking water, power, irrigation and communication. The prophet Jeremiah questioned going to 'Egypt, to drink the waters of the Nile' and 'to Assyria, to drink the waters of the Euphrates' (Jer. 2.18), and the writer of Exodus describes how the daughter of Pharaoh 'came down to bathe at the river' (Exod. 2.5). Rivers irrigate vegetation – as in Genesis, 'a river flows out of Eden to water the garden' (Gen. 2.10) – and so contribute to commerce: 'your revenue was the grain of Shihor, the harvest of the Nile' (Isa. 23.3). The majority of the world's towns and cities are located next to rivers or lakes. They bring in the drinking water and flush out the sewage.

The aesthetic value of water, and particularly how light dances over it and causes reflection, has been an inspiration for painters, poets and writers. Sir Walter Scott (1771–1832), the Scottish historical novelist, playwright and poet, celebrated Loch Katrine and its surrounding Trossach landscape in his poem 'The Lady of the Lake'; later, with the corresponding rise in tourism to the area, Gerard Manley Hopkins (1844–89) wrote his 1881 poem 'Inversnaid', which captures in vivid detail and sharp focus the drama of a waterfall:

> This darksome burn, horseback brown,
> His rollrock highroad roaring down,
> In coop and in comb the fleece of his foam
> Flutes and low to the lake falls home.
>
> A windpuff-bonnet of fawn-froth
> Turns and twindles over the broth
> Of a pool so pitchblack, fell-frowning,
> It rounds and rounds Despair to drowning.
>
> Degged with dew, dappled with dew,
> Are the groins of the braes that the brook
>   treads through,
> Wiry heathpacks, flitches of fern,
> And the beadbonny ash that sits over the burn.
>
> What would the world be, once bereft
> Of wet and wildness? Let them be left,
> O let them be left, wildness and wet;
> Long live the weeds and the wilderness yet.[2]

Water has also been used as a symbol for mystery and the unknown. The desolation of the north Kent marshes was recreated by Charles Dickens (1812–70) in his novel *Great Expectations* as the setting for Pip's childhood. This 'wild country of marsh and mist' is used to symbolize danger and foreboding, with Pip nearly being murdered there, then, after receiving his fortune, having to cross the marshes on his way to London, raising the tension for the reader.

Fresh water is a scarce resource, covering only 1 per cent of the earth's surface. Rivers are in daily danger of pollution, over-exploitation, damming, and being waste sinks, and these issues affect thousands of people living near their banks whose lives are entwined with the flow of the river. According to the World Conservation Union, 34 per cent of fish species, mostly from freshwater areas, are threatened with extinction.[3] The interconnections are immense, with river systems underscoring the whole development and prosperity of regions. For the fishermen of Maria Ribeira (mentioned in Chapter 3) their entire way of life depends on the river Amazon. They call it their father (the surrounding rainforest is their mother), that 'gives the best to his children'. Its water provides not only bathing and drinking water, but transport, in dug-out canoes and the noisy, onomatopoeically named putt-putt boats plying their river taxi trade, and also much of the community's food. I recall going out into the river with a local fisherman, João Paulo, and catching 16 small fish; but the day before he had caught only four fish. One day the family has little food to go round, the next it is a feast for family and neighbours. But João Paulo, now in his thirties, reckons that there is now much less fish than when he was a boy. He and other local fishermen blame this on the multinational trawlers sonar-chasing shoals in the Amazon. They take the largest fish and throw back dead the smaller ones that have long been the local people's staple catch.

Rivers can also be dangerous and foreboding landscapes, with strong currents, rapids and waterfalls, and there is a fear of falling in and losing control. The writer of Psalm 69, overwhelmed by difficulties, speaks of some of these sinking places: 'Save me, O God, for the waters have come up to my neck. I sink in deep mire, where there is no foothold: I have come into deep waters, and the flood sweeps over me' (Ps. 69.1–2). In another Psalm we hear, 'The floods have lifted up, O LORD, the floods have lifted up their voice; the floods lift up their roaring' (Ps. 93.3), though the writer goes on to observe that God's power is even greater than that of untamed nature. Living near rivers, especially with the unpredictability of weather, can bring a risk of flooding and the resulting washing away of livelihoods, possessions and life itself. 'How close is your property to a lake or river?' the insurance company routinely asks. For the vast majority of the world's population, this question is immaterial. Life and possessions are not insured and daily life is a gamble and a trial. For the people living in the lakeside communities of Bodal and Nesdal in the Lodalen Valley of Norway, 100 years ago, this risk became a reality. Rockslides from the Ramnefjellet mountain occurred in 1905, and again in 1936, sending tidal waves that swept along the valley; in total 134 people were killed, the disasters thus affecting two generations. To this day the remains of a boat can be seen, washed high above the lake. Yet, we also hear of a God who does not desert us, 'When you pass through the waters, I will be with you; and through the rivers, they shall not overwhelm you' (Isa. 43.2).

Opportunity and risk come together in the first few words of Genesis: 'in the beginning when God created the heavens and the earth, the earth was a formless void and darkness covered the face of the deep, while a wind from God swept over the face of the waters' (Gen. 1.1–2). The poetic language provides an insight that from the first moment of creation, as in every repeating creative moment since, both the opportunities and the risks were, and are, immense. The Spirit animated the waters and the very act of creation unfolded in a dynamism of wonder. Out of water life emerged.

Later in Genesis, in the Noah story (Gen. 8.8–12), the dove flies out from the ark to glide over the waters to see if they are receding. First it comes back with nothing in its beak. Like today's pigeon-fanciers, Noah sends the bird out again, and this time it comes back with a little twig. To be sure, it goes out again, for a third time, and it does not return. Perhaps it had begun to build a nest? In Scripture, the next dove to be encountered over water is when Jesus enters into the waters of the Jordan. This can be seen as Noah's dove coming back at last, descending from heaven, with the words of affirmation that were to equip Jesus in his ministry. In the time of Noah, sin was drowned in water. In Jesus' baptism the dove symbolizes that out of that water has come a new way of being God's people. The fact that the Gospel writers also speak about the Spirit over the waters links the moment to the beginning of Genesis. Jesus' baptism is being cast as a story of re-creation; out of water we are created and we are continually drawn back to the promise that we are to be the people God would have us be.

The river Jordan, which rises on Mount Hermon and flows south through the Sea of Galilee and 65 miles further on to the Dead Sea, is a fairly insignificant river in terms of the world's hydrology. Naaman, the Syrian, was to complain when Elisha commanded him to wash in it: 'Are not Abana and Pharpar, the rivers of Damascus, better than all the waters of Israel?' (2 Kings 5.12). It was, however, a natural barrier and a political border, only crossed without difficulty at fords, due to its thick wooded banks (Jer. 49.19).

Today the Jordan river is a muddy stream and something of a disappointment when viewed from the pilgrims' tour bus. In many places its banks are littered with the memories of past conflicts, and metal signs warn that the area still contains land mines. According to a report by *National Geographic* magazine,[4] the Jordan has lost 90 per cent of its water flow over the last five decades, leaving one-time beach resorts on the Sea of Galilee and at the Dead Sea high and dry. The lower waters therefore contain little fresh water, 'bearing instead a toxic brew of saline water and liquid waste that ranges from raw sewage to agricultural runoff, fed into the river's vein like some murky infusion of tainted blood'.[5] This is because Israel has diverted the waters towards its cities and farms, irrigating former arid areas so that the desert might bloom with cash crops. This is yet another source of tension between Israelis and Palestinians and the wider region. Palestinians in occupied areas have been prevented from digging deep wells for themselves, thus having to rely upon shallow wells and natural springs that dry up in the early months of the year. This leaves them with no choice but to purchase water from Israel, 'for about a dollar a cubic yard – in effect buying back the water that's been taken out from under them by [Israeli] pumps, which also lower the water table and affect Palestinian springs and wells'.[6] The fight over the waters of the Jordan illustrates that future wars may well have issues around water security at their heart.

For Jesus and his contemporaries, the Jordan was not just an ordinary river. This was the river that was crossed by Joshua as he brought the Israelites into the Promised Land. It marked the end of slavery and wandering, and brought a refreshing vision of a new start. When John the Baptist stood knee-deep in the river, he began calling to the crowds, saying that it was likewise time to change their minds and follow in a new direction. From within that landscape, so pregnant with meaning, he says to Jesus that it is time again for a new start and a new vision. The Israelites were again in slavery, but now it is a Roman power that oppresses them and is routing them. Their leadership is wandering and lacks integrity, having gone off the mark through being so bound up within their strict moral codes. So Jesus chooses that moment to slip into the waters of his people's history and to be carried by the flow of God into a future of sorrow but ultimately new hope.

In our baptism we too are united with Jesus in this journey. We too come through the waters of baptism re-created and re-promised. Both are God's actions to us and ours to God. We are re-created as part of the family of God, freed from sin, equipped to serve and to respond to God's Word. This is not, then, some very personal moment, but a time for the whole Church to rejoice in the gifts it gives and receives. We are also re-promised that God is with us, accompanying us as we slip into the River of Life, as we add our own 'yes' to the 'yes' that God has always said. We are reminded of this most movingly as we renew our baptismal vows at the Easter liturgy. As we stand as witnesses to the re-creating power of God that is evidenced by the stone rolled away, the linen bands folded in the empty tomb, so we are drawn into the creativity of God as the Easter flame burns, at first in total darkness, with its promise that there is hope. 'For he is risen indeed, Alleluia!' brings a new flow of energy and life within us. As we are sprinkled with water as a sign of our baptism, or our foreheads are marked in water with the sign of the cross, so we step back into that flow of the River of Life which is given to us through Jesus' life, passion, death and resurrection. Little wonder, with all this liturgical signi-ficance, that this was the service at which, in the early church, new converts were baptized and those who had become estranged from the community were received back.

In the final chapter of Revelation (22.1ff.), John the Divine is shown by his angel tour guide a river flowing through the main street of the heavenly city. The 'river of the water of life' is its name. The river is lined with trees, which we have already climbed in Chapter 3, and it comes from the throne of God. Standing on its bank, John describes it as sparkling as bright as crystal. The throne is the source of all power, unlike John's earthly experience where all power stemmed from Rome, and the river, with the leaves of the trees, bring nourishment, regeneration and healing for all who draw near. Of course, we recognize the imagery. Here the river that watered the Garden of Eden wells up in the heavenly city to continue that story of nourishment. The difference now is that those who were banished from the garden are welcomed home.

The vision also links with Ezekiel's prophecy of Jerusalem's future aquatics. Among the prophets' various writings, Ezekiel's vision (Ezek. 47.1–12; see also Zech. 14.8) of new rivers springing up in Jerusalem is one of the more obscure. A river is to well up in Jerusalem from underneath the Temple and become ever deeper the further it flows. One part is to flow down to the Mediterranean, the other in the opposite direction to the Dead Sea. There it will bring fresh water to that salted environment, where only a few obscure micro-organisms can live, so that it becomes a fisherman's paradise. The river nourishes the trees along the banks of the river and the trees produce fruit. Everything will live where the river goes.

Those who read this passage with a literal understanding go to great lengths to describe how massive geological and geographical changes to the landscape will be necessary to enable this to happen. A more metaphorical interpretation sees the waters as signifying the gospel of Christ, spreading, like the marks on a Jerusalem cross or the carved crosses on an altar, to the four corners of the world. Such an interpretation sees the risen Jesus as the Temple, and from his pierced side flow living waters that increase in volume and gather pace the further they flow. Some of these waters are ankle-deep and easily understood; others require a deeper search; and some are quite beyond our depth, where we must, like Paul, simply adore the deep.[7] The metaphor helps us to see the Church as a River of Life that can bring healing to the communities that it serves.

At St Paul's Chapel in Lower Manhattan, this was seen strikingly in the wake of the atrocities of 9/11. The church, in the next block to the twin towers of the World Trade Center, once dwarfed by them and seemingly insignificant, opened its doors to the rescue workers, having remarkably escaped undamaged when the towers collapsed. For eight months hundreds of volunteers worked 12-hour shifts to serve meals and prepare beds. Even George Washington's private pew had its hallowed heritage status removed, and became the chiropody clinic to soothe sore feet. In that place, through prayers, music, therapy and space, the river of Christian healing balm was present to people caught up in the most gruesome of tasks.

The Church has the potential to be this river that carries the love of God in its wake so that all may drink deeply. The interesting thing about Ezekiel's imagery is that the rivers are always flowing outwards to bring abundant life. Even the Dead Sea will teem with fish. If the Temple is the Church, the water is not there for its own nourishment but instead is bringing refreshment and growth to those who have no part in it. As such the River of Life here is not something personal, or even within a narrow communal setting, but is over-flowing all that might hold it back so as to be for the good of all. Despite our best efforts at containment and institutionalization, God's ever-flowing gift continues to flow out into the widest and darkest of places.

Sitting on the banks of a river reminds us that the Christian pilgrimage is about allowing oneself to enter into this continuing flow of God's love; to dive into, or slip into, the river of the water of life. There are calm, deep waters where one can float serenely, as well as the shallows where the going is easy, like the still waters we are led beside in Psalm 23. Ahead may be rocky rapids where no toe-hold can be found and you are tossed around, or an estuary where life's course goes out to a wider horizon and some new challenge ahead. Do we go with the flow, excited by the journey and its unexpected twists and turns, seeing these as God-given opportunities? Or do we sit on the banks, remembering the past and weeping like those in exile in Babylon: 'By the rivers of Babylon, there we sat down and there we wept, when we remembered Zion' (Ps. 137.1)? Or do we fight it the whole time? Perhaps we are not as trusting as Annie Taylor, who in October 1901 became the first person to survive a barrel ride down the Niagara Falls, suffering just bumps and bruises, or the subsequent 1911 survivor, Bobby Leach, who had the misfortune later to slip on an orange peel and die from complications to his injuries!

There is a Buddhist story that fits this theme of journeying well. It talks of an ancient spiritual teacher who meditated each day at the edge of a river. He was approached one day by a student who asked him how meditating on the bank of a river could lead to enlightenment. The master smiled and told the student that sitting on the bank of a river is the same as paying attention to one's life. Like a river, life simply flows. It can bring us pleasure, but if we try to grasp or hang onto the pleasure too hard we will cause ourselves suffering, because like a river, life will eventually take the pleasure away.

The teacher recalled how in entering the River of Life we enter into opportunity and risk. There are times when that river will cause us suffering and pain. Holding on, we travel further, but in letting go we enter a new hope and, in time, the scenery changes. All we can do, said the teacher, is sit with what the River of Life brings us, and learn the lessons that we are meant to learn. After some time had passed, the student bowed to the teacher and continued on his journey.

Rivers have, in recent decades, formed the backdrop to the rejuvenation of some of our inner cities. Town centres, for which waterways were useful merely for sewage, transportation and industry, turned their backs on rivers and wharfs in favour of elegant streets paid for, in many cases, by the collective wealth that the river trade had brought. Through the regenerative spirit, cities like Bristol, Newcastle upon Tyne and Gateshead have turned again to face the river. With new bridges, public attractions, and civic buildings the Avon and the Tyne have been enhanced. During the day they are the destination for business and tourism and in the evening have a vibrant night-life. In such places the river has become a symbol of new life and a sense of future hope. There are clear linkages here with a similar theme of the river illustrating God's rejuvenating spirit within the Judaeo-Christian tradition. 'I will open rivers on the bare heights, and fountains in the midst of the valleys,' wrote Isaiah. 'I will make the wilderness a pool of water, and the dry land springs of water' (Isa. 41.18).

There is ample evidence of water springs being sacred places. The word 'well' appears in the names of many places, such as Wilton in Somerset, Welton in Yorkshire, Willesden in Middlesex, and the hamlet of Holywell in Northumberland. Some place names suggest the patronage of or connection to a saint, such as Hinderwell near Whitby, a corruption of St Hilda's Well. In Derbyshire there is a tradition of well-dressing, which celebrates the stories of these special sites in floral displays. Nick Mayhew Smith's book about 500 of Britain's holiest sites tells us that about one-quarter of them are the holy wells that dot the landscape.[8] Many villages have holy wells nearby, each with a distinctive name and folklore attached to them. Wells are often seen as places of healing. This relates to two stories in John's Gospel where Jesus heals. In one he restores the ability of a lame man to walk. For years this man had been waiting by the pool of Bethesda so as to be the first to get in when the waters were stirred up, a sign of an impending miracle (John 5.2–9). The other is about a man born blind; in a rather stomach-turning detail, Jesus spits on the ground to make mud which he rubs on the man's eyes before telling him to wash in the pool of Siloam. When he comes out of the water, he can see (John 9.1–7).

Springs are also impossible to destroy. As Nick Mayhew Smith has reminded us, 'You can smash a statue or dig up a saint's grave, but you'd have to geologically re-engineer much of the Peak District to knock out St Ann's holy well in Buxton, which gushes out around 10 litres per second.'[9] So some medieval churches and shrines were deliberately built near or over springs venerated earlier by pagans possibly because it was found to be simpler to do so rather than refute their supposed powers when it was discovered that they could not be destroyed. At Wolsingham, in County Durham, a holy well is covered by a stone building with a barrel ceiling and slate roof, and the pool of water fills the whole building. The gate carries the names of St Aelric and St Godric, local saints, but their connection to the well is lost in time. The well, like countless others, was a place of community gathering where not only water but gossip flowed, a tradition we also find in the story of Jesus meeting the Samaritan woman at Jacob's well (John 4.4–42). The woman has come in the heat of the day, probably to avoid the taunts of others about her being someone outside the community and having a dubious past. Jesus, breaking the strict moral code of his day about engagement, uses the moment to offer her not stale water from a well but something incredibly more – the 'water of life'. When the penny does begin to drop, she leaves behind her jar of water, the symbol of her daily grind, forgets her thirst, and hurries back to her community in the city with the exciting news of her encounter. In such a way she becomes a spring for others, uttering words of invitation to her peers because she realizes that this vibrant living water cannot be contained. Echoing Jesus' own invitation to his disciples, she says, 'Come and see'. It is an invitation that leads to Jesus staying with them for two days, breaking all kinds of further taboos; he demonstrates his understanding that all enmity is over and offers them the chance to drink from the fountain of life, overflowing with generosity and inclusion like the streams that 'run to the sea, but the sea is not full' (Eccles. 1.7).

River landscapes provide a metaphor for the spiritual journey and, as we have explored, draw us back to our own baptism as we set our stroke within the flow of the River of Life. I remember being with a group of pilgrims gathered round a pool of water at the historical site of Caesarea Philippi where some of the headwaters of the river Jordan emerge. The spring was so powerful that the surface of the water was in continuous rapid motion. We renewed our baptismal vows and drenched ourselves with the cool water. It ran down our necks and we felt refreshed in so many different ways. The words of Tertullian (*c*.160–*c*.220), a theologian in the early church, came to mind: 'We, being like little fishes, as Jesus Christ is our great Fish, begin our life in the water, and only while we abide in the water are we safe and sound.'[10]

5

Mountain

Ben Hope is the most northern Scottish mountain over the magical height of 3,000 feet (914 metres), which makes it a 'Munro'. The list of names in this group of 283 mountains was assembled by Sir Hugh Munro in 1891. I first climbed Ben Hope as a seven-year-old with my father, the first of a number of Munros in the bag. I can still recall aspects of that journey, especially eating the celebratory summit Mars bar, closely followed by being enveloped in a cloud of midges on the descent. Slap dead one of the little biters on your face and it is as if a thousand turn up for its funeral! Some years ago my father and I returned to Ben Hope, this time introducing my own seven-year-old to the mountain. There were many things that made it a day to remember, not least the nostalgic power of memory and family story. It's a hard climb, starting at near sea level, but from the summit on that bright blue May day we looked out with eagle's eyes across the northern landscape to the sea beyond, and to the other mountains of Klibreck, Arkle and Foinaven as if they were only a leapfrog away. The landscape writer Robert MacFarlane, who experienced this mountain in the snow, anticipated it being a place that rang true to Wallace Stegner's phrase of feeling a sense of 'bigness outside yourself'.[1] Time stood still for us on the summit as we lay on the rocks basking like lizards in the sun, feeling tiny in this great landscape, the cool air flowing over us. There was a sense of open space, of remoteness, even a sense of freedom. If only I could flap my arms and take off to soar on the up-currents and swoop down into the valley below that was marked by the remains of a fortified broch, home of an Iron Age community that once looked up to the heights of this mountain. How did they see the mountain, I wonder? Come a different season and they, like myself, might have looked on it differently. There have been times when I have been scared in the mountains, clinging to rocks and keeping myself as near the ground as possible so as not to be blown off a ridge by the wind, or enveloped in thick fog and having to put all my trust in the metal needlepoint of my compass to avoid dangerous cliffs. Mountain landscapes need to be treated with respect, care and caution.

Until 200 years or so ago, this caution amounted to fear. The young wealthy aristocrats on their Grand Tour of Europe passed through the Alps but, according to contemporary accounts, kept the curtains of their carriage windows firmly drawn so as not to see the ominous view. They found the mountains to be frightening and unfamiliar, undesirable and repellent – monstrous excrescences of warts, pimples and blisters on the face of the earth. They chose to look at mountainous landscapes through the safety of the soothing Claude mirror. This small handheld device allowed travellers to stand with their backs to the landscape and hold up the curved mirror in order to see a landscape not so much in the raw but carefully framed. It was named after Claude Lorrain, who we met in Chapter 1, a popular late Renaissance painter of idealized landscapes. The mirror was prepared in such a way that the viewer saw a slightly darkened landscape, with a reduced colour and a simplified tonal range, as if painted over with a varnish, which was in the typical style of a Claude Lorrain painting. Clergyman Thomas West explained, in his *A Guide to the Lakes*, written in 1778:

> When the objects are great and near, it removes them to a due distance, and shows them in the soft colours of nature, and in the most regular perspective the eye can perceive or science demonstrate. The person using it ought always to turn his back to the object that he views. It should be suspended by the upper part of the case and the landscape will then be seen in the glass, by holding it a little to the right or the left (as the position of the parts to be viewed require) and the face screened from the sun.[2]

William Wordsworth (1770–1850) was one of those who broke through this idea of landscape needing to be tamed into a cosy picture. In his autobiographical poem *The Prelude*, Wordsworth, rather than simply *looking* at what was there, began to *see* it; and so he conveyed something of the awe of the Lakeland landscape.

> The bound of the horizon, a huge Cliff,
> As if with voluntary power instinct,
> Uprear'd its head: I struck and struck again,
> And, growing still in stature, the huge Cliff
> Rose up between me and the stars, and still,
> With measur'd motion, like a living thing,
> Strode after me . . .[3]

Because this way of seeing landscape was new to Wordsworth it disturbed him, as the unknown usually will, but slowly he was to open up a new way of viewing mountains as places of grandeur and magnificence. In later years, though, he tried to guard this landscape from the sight of the masses by opposing investment that would increase Lakeland tourism. 'Mountains remain symbols to Wordsworth and his generation of that "more beyond" to which imagination persistently aspires, of the eternity and infinity that are the unattainable goals of the imagination,' commented Marjorie Hope Nicholson (1894–1981) in her book *Mountain Gloom and Mountain Glory.*[4] In this review of the work of poets and writers she argued that this new way of looking at mountains happened within a 50-year period as a result of a radical shift in understanding about the structure of the earth and the universe of which it is part.

The spiritual qualities of mountains are recognized within ecosystem cultural services as having a 'peculiarly evocative nature', where the 'sight of a peak reaching toward the clean blue heights of the sky lifts the mind and spirit, conjuring up visions of a higher, more perfect realm of existence'.[5] As well as these aesthetic spiritual qualities, mountains are regarded as sacred places, home to both good and evil spirits, by different communities. Followers of St Francis of Assisi (*c.*1182–1226) established Mount La Verna in central Italy as a sacred mountain; it has a route dotted with stations of the cross leading up to a Calvary. It was on this mountain, during a 40-day retreat, that Francis received his stigmata, his hagiography recording that one day he looked out of his cell:

> considering the form of the mountain, and marvelling at the exceeding clefts and caverns in the mighty rocks, he betook himself to prayer, and then it was revealed to him by God that those clefts, so marvellous, had been miraculously made at the hour of the Passion of Christ, when, according to the gospel, the rocks were rent asunder. And this, God willed, should manifestly appear on the mount of La Verna, because there the Passion of our Lord Jesus Christ was to be renewed, through love and pity, in the soul of St Francis.[6]

Making the pilgrimage up the mountain, visiting chapels with life-size figures along the way, not only brought the penitent closer to St Francis' suffering but drew them nearer to the mystery of God. This, like sacred mountains in other religious traditions, was seen as the *axis mundi*, a place where earth and heaven meet, where humans and God meet. Such sacred mountains have the reputation of being sources of blessings, which can be invoked for such things as water, life, healing, health and well-being. The fact that mountains are often shrouded in swirling mist leads to an aura of mystery, the clouds concealing a deeper reality. Add to this storms, punctuated with flashes of lightning and crashes of thunder, and mountains take on the mantle of being awesome supernatural places.

We see a fine example of this in the writings of George Mallory (1886–1924), perhaps the first person to climb Mount Everest, depending on whether he died on his ascent or descent of the world's highest mountain. In all he tried three times to conquer Everest, so possessed was he by the beauty of the mountain. He was able to capture the mountain's sense of mystery and seductive power, with what could not be seen being more compelling to the imagination than what could:

We were now able to make out almost exactly where Everest should be; but the clouds were dark in that direction. We gazed at them intently through field glasses as though by some miracle we might pierce the veil. Presently the miracle happened. We caught the gleam of snow behind the grey mists. A whole group of mountains began to appear in gigantic fragments. Mountain shapes are often fantastic seen through a mist; these were like the wildest creation of a dream. A preposterous triangular lump rose out of the depths; its edge came leaping up at an angle of about seventy degrees and ended nowhere. To the left a black serrated crest was hanging in the sky incredibly. Gradually, very gradually, we saw the great mountainsides and glaciers and arêtes, now one fragment, now another through the floating rifts, until far higher in the sky than imagination had dared to suggest, the white summit of Everest appeared. And in this series of partial glimpses we had seen a whole; we were able to piece together the fragments, to interpret the dream. However much might remain to be understood the centre had a clear meaning as one mountain shape, the shape of Everest.[7]

The United Nations' Millennium Ecosystem Assessment recognized the importance of mountains in people's lives. It concluded that 'since the environment itself contributes to the efficacy of a mountain as a place of revelation, transformation or inspiration, people will have reason to do what they can to maintain its biological integrity'. This motivates both the environmental movement and 'the measures traditional societies have taken to set aside and protect their sacred mountains'.[8] We see an example of this in the thought of the Greek Orthodox monks and hermits of Mount Athos. They refer to their sacred peninsula as the 'Garden of the Mother of God' and see their own role as being gardeners or stewards entrusted with the task of caring for the natural environment of the Holy Mountain.

The Irish-born, Scottish-based theologian Fr Noel O'Donoghue wrote about the sense of God being present on the mountain, in the context of the poetry of Kathleen Raine. His book *The Mountain Behind the Mountain* used as its title an expression of hers:

The mountain behind or within the mountain is not the perfect or ideal mountain in some Platonic sense ... [It] is neither an ideal nor a mythical mountain, nor is it exactly a holy or sacred mountain made sacred by theophany or transfiguration. No, it is a very ordinary, very physical mountain, a place of sheep and kine [cattle], of peat, and of streams that one might fish in or bathe in on a summer's day. It is an elemental mountain, of earth and air and water and fire, of sun and moon and wind and rain. What makes it special for me and for the people from which I come is that it is a place of Presence and a place of presences. Only those who can perceive this in its ordinariness can encounter the mountain behind the mountain.[9]

In such a way mountain landscapes are sublime, with the capacity to surprise us as a new vista comes into view or as they capture and reflect light. The Aberdonian hillwalker, poet and writer Nan Shepherd (1893–1981) described something of the magic of the Cairngorms in her book *The Living Mountain*. On the bookshelf of mountain-writing her work is unusual not least because the genre is dominated by men and their aim for the summit. She mourned the loss of society's contact with the landscape of the mountain and discovered that it was through the metaphysical rhythm of walking that she found 'the still centre of being'. This opened a way in for her, in a process that took many years, to a greater understanding of the mountain where 'everything became good to me, its contours, its colours, its water and rock, flowers and birds'. 'It is a journey into Being,' she wrote, 'for as I penetrate more deeply into the mountain's life, I penetrate more deeply into my own.'[10] This, Belden Lane commented, is what social psychologist Mihaly Csikszentmihalyi termed 'flow':

> the holistic sensation we experience whenever we act with total involvement . . . one action following another without need for conscious intervention. There is a loss of ego, a diminished sense of control. Little distinction is made between the self and the environment, as everything moves together in unforced harmony.[11]

As Christians we are aware that it is the journey, the meander on the mountain, that is as important as reaching the summit, perhaps more important.

It is a shame that over recent years there has been a reversal to the earlier fear of mountains, in British society at least, with them increasingly being seen as dangerous.[12] Following some high-profile and tragic accidents we heavily guard our children from experiencing wild nature while at the same time mountain rescue teams report an increase in adults venturing out ill-equipped. Without maps, a compass and adequate clothing, as well as the necessary knowledge and planning, it is little wonder that people are not prepared for dealing with the dangers that these landscapes contain. Richard Louv, in his best-selling book *Last Child in the Woods*,[13] described from a North American perspective how a whole generation of children has lost contact with nature; the reins have been drawn in so far that the young no longer have free-range play, and Louv recorded the impact that this is having on a variety of developmental measures including their weight, knowledge, creativity and spirituality.

There are certainly plenty of places to explore, as mountain areas cover a quarter of the earth's surface. Like other landscapes, though, they are under pressure for development. Having long been inaccessible and remote places that kept all but the hardiest away, and maintained indigenous mountain populations as distinct cultures, the pressure to mine and extract, to plunder and gain is increasing. These landscapes are rich in biodiversity, given the vertical diversity of plant and animal populations that thrive in the range of different climatic and soil habitats. The equivalent range of diversity is separated by thousands of miles on the plain. Mountains are the primary source of water for half of all people. They are also the first places affected by climate change, as they are already at the extremes of life.

Some mountain landscapes have already long since disappeared. Others have been manipulated so as to cause disfiguration, colonizing summits with restaurants and amusement arcades to provide tourist income. Simon Schama talked about the huge carvings on the cliffs of Mount Rushmore, of the heads of four past United States Presidents by Gutzon Borglum, as the 'ultimate colonization of nature by culture, the alteration of landscape to manscape'.[14] Two decades before they were carved, John Muir had died despondently, having failed the previous year, in 1913, to save Hetch Hetchy Valley, Yosemite's neighbour, from being dammed to provide water for a burgeoning San Francisco that was recovering from its devastating 1906 earthquake. In frustration he wrote at the time:

> These temple destroyers, devotees of ravaging commercialism, seem to have a perfect contempt for Nature, and, instead of lifting their eyes to the God of the mountains, lift them to the Almighty Dollar. Dam Hetch Hetchy! As well dam for water-tanks the people's cathedrals and churches, for no holier temple has ever been consecrated by the heart of man.[15]

Construction of the dam was completed in 1923 and the valley was flooded.

Throughout the biblical record we find mountains being places of theophany. It was on Mount Sinai, or Horeb as it is also known, that Moses, having fled Egypt and while tending the flock of his father-in-law Jethro, encountered the voice of God at the burning bush (Exod. 3.1–6). Sinai is a harsh and fearsome environment, untamed and desolate, a place on the edge, where life is frugal and death is never far away, and this was the first of a series of moments of theophany that Moses had on the mountain. God's presence at the burning bush, which in its sacramental nature served to fill Moses with such awe and fear that he hid his face, also equipped him for his task. He was to be sent 'to Pharaoh to bring my people, the Israelites, out of Egypt' (Exod. 3.10); God had 'heard [my people's] cry' (Exod. 3.7) where they lived under the yoke of slavery. Moses was to bring them into a land flowing with milk and honey.

Later, having asked to see God's face, Moses glimpses only the shadow of God's grandeur from a hiding place in the cleft of the rock (Exod. 33.21–23). As we shall see elsewhere, God is met in emptiness, and avoids all our efforts to prepackage and giftwrap him. Belden Lane has remarked that Sinai's impulse is 'to empty us of inadequate images, to destroy idolatries, to cut through all false conceptions of the holy. It boldly deconstructs every human attempt to capture and contain God who dwells in thick darkness.'[16]

Mount Sinai's physical location, as with many places in the Bible, is contested. While some scholars favour a more northerly place, the traditional site is placed near Jebel Musa at the southern end of the Sinai peninsula. The orthodox monastery of St Catherine (officially called the Monastery of the Transfiguration), was founded in the year 527 in the mountain's shadow and is said to be built around the site of the burning bush. Pilgrims remove their shoes as a reminder of God's command to Moses that this was holy ground. A shrub in the enclosure is venerated as being the surviving bush, and a chapel has been built over its roots; it is said that any attempt to take cuttings from the bush to plant elsewhere will always fail. Egeria, a fourth-century pilgrim from Spain, saw this bush in her travels:

> Our way took us to the head of this valley because there the holy men had many cells, and there is also a church there at the place of the Bush (which is still alive and sprouting) . . . the Bush itself is in front of the church in a very pretty garden which has plenty of excellent water. Near by you are also shown the place where holy Moses was standing when God said to him, 'Undo the fastening of thy shoes', and so on . . . we had a prayer in the church, and also in the garden by the Bush, and as usual the appropriate passage was read from the book of Moses. Then, because it was late, we had our meal with the holy men in the garden near the Bush, and stayed there for the night.[17]

On the mountain we see the authentication of Moses as mediator between God and his people, as the Lord's presence on the mountain is experienced in cloud, smoke, fire, the sounds of a trumpet and thunder (Exod. 19.16). Moses' repeated ascent and descent builds up drama and tension in the story in preparation for the giving of the law. When Moses finally enters the cloud covering the mountain, he spends 40 days and 40 nights in its swirling mist listening to God (Exod. 24.12–18). Having received the Ten Commandments, on his return he is shocked to find that his people are worshipping a golden calf that they have made. He throws the two stone tablets containing the law onto the floor, smashing them in his disgust. Later, when Moses receives new tablets from God he descends the mountain with his face shining (Exod. 34.29), and in order to alleviate the people's fear he places a veil over his face when he addresses them. St Paul picks up the theme of the veil (2 Cor. 12–18), talking about how we as disciples of Jesus have no need of the veil because by looking on God we are 'being transformed into the same image from one degree of glory to another'. Despite the focus being on Moses, it must not be forgotten that the whole people of Israel were called to worship at the mountain, and experienced the presence of God in their midst. This joint experience of God helped to form them as a new nation and prepared them as a community for their mission.

This story has inspired pilgrims to make precarious journeys from one mountaintop to another searching out the site of the theophany. Simon Schama recorded the work of the compiler of a twelfth-century geographical *Descriptio*, which provided invaluable information for intrepid explorers into Sinai, who wrote:

Of Sinai it is stated (and it is true) that each Sabbath a heavenly fire surrounds it but does not burn it, and whoever touches it is not harmed. It appears many times, like white blankets going round the mountain with an easy motion, and sometimes it descends with a terrible sound which can hardly be tolerated and the most holy servants of Christ hide themselves in caves and cells of the monastery [of St Catherine].[18]

Years after Moses, the great prophet Elijah won his contest with the priests of Baal on Mount Carmel. Carmel was significant in a number of ways. As a mountain it was expected to be a place that would exhibit the coming of the Lord in cloud and fire, but it was also a fertile place, topped with a forest, and claimed as the home stadium of Baal, the god of fertility, rainfall and new growth. Thanks to God's intervention in sending fire to consume his water-soaked bull offering (1 Kings 18.38), the God of Elijah is seen to be the living God, in comparison with Baal who manages no intervention. In triumph Elijah has the priests massacred down by the riverbank (1 Kings 18.40). Queen Jezebel, a devoted follower of Baal, is livid and vows in turn to kill this troublesome prophet. Frightened, Elijah runs for his life, leaving the city and heading for the desert. Out in the desert everything seems lost. He has withdrawn completely from society. It is as if all his work has come to an end and, with echoes back to Hagar, he curls up on the desert floor under a broom tree to sleep, ready to give up and to die. The text is full of much historical imagery. There is a 40-day journey in the desert that links to the Israelites' 40 years of wandering in the wilderness, and it is a journey without food and water, like Moses' 40 days on the mountain (Exod. 34.28). As the passage progresses so we find that Elijah, like Moses, experiences the presence of God, and does so on the same mountain, as Horeb and Sinai are one and the same, in a way that he was not expecting. Still in hiding, he first finds shelter in a cave. In another linkage with the past some commentators suggest that the cave may be the cleft in the rock where Moses saw God's glory pass by (Exod. 33.21–23). Wherever he was, Elijah is confused and unsure of his future and in need of insight and instruction. He is asked a soul-searching question: 'What are you doing here?' He is still smarting from all that has happened. Annoyed by Israel's loss of faith, and filled with his own sense of self-pity and feeling of God's abandonment, he cannot see that it was God who led him to this place. It is at this moment that he is told to come out of the cave, as the Lord will pass by.

Having seen the manifestation of God in fire on Mount Carmel, Elijah's religious and cultural milieu would have expected that it would be through the forces of nature that he would experience God, especially those symbols of God experienced during the exodus. Outside the cave, rocks begin to shatter in the wind, and you can imagine them danger-ously cascading down the mountainside, chips breaking off that could have flown into the mouth of the cave like grenades (1 Kings 19.8–13). But God is not encountered there. An earthquake shakes Elijah's feet and would have left him feeling dizzy and disoriented. But God is not encountered there, nor in the fire that sweeps over the mountain, hot, crackling and licking up the rockface. Then, rejecting all classic religious imagery, comes a faint whisper, a still, small voice, and Elijah can respond only by covering his face with his mantle garment, the one that one day he would pass on to Elisha. He encounters God in a way that is beyond understanding and language. The 'faint whisper' has also been translated as a 'crushing silence'. This seems to me to convey something of the deep silences that are encountered in mountains. Whatever it was, it changed Elijah, deepening his knowledge of God, and equipping him to go back to his life as a prophet and to a ministry that involved the anointing of kings and the stirring up of a rebellion against Ahab and Jezebel.

Mount Sinai teaches us about the elusiveness of God and how God comes often not in the sensational and spectacular but in unexpected ways. If we approach a landscape expecting a theophany we will be disappointed and simply end up with an enjoyable aesthetic experience. It is when we least expect things, when we let go and live in the moment of the mountains, devoid of the clutter and noise of our lives, that we too might hear that still, small voice out there and deep within us. 'Jesus Christ, who is the Word of God, came forth out of silence,' wrote St Ignatius of Antioch (*c.*35–*c.*107), and that is often how we still encounter him. In making time to listen, we can find the goal of our searching. Our commitment is renewed and we are resourced for the next stage of our pilgrimage.

The passage offers us something in our struggle to understand where God is in natural disasters. When the enormity of an earthquake, flood, hurricane or fire hits our TV news, so the human stories of loss pierce our soul. The anguish and heartache of people who have lost loved ones, possessions and livelihoods soon prompts the question, 'Where was God?' Perhaps taking this story of Elijah might help us, not with glib answers that help no one (and can even cause greater suffering), but by wondering whether we can begin what can only be an incomplete answer with the suggestion that God was not in the wind, the earthquake, or the fire, but God is in the silence. Silence is often the experience of people in the split-second after a disaster. That time of the gulp of air before the crying and the sirens begin. In that silence, when the birds don't sing, is a pause, a waiting. Is that God, I wonder, in the midst of it all, the first to be mourning and crying, the first to be waiting with us, longing for healing, wholeness and *tikkun olam*, the Jewish phrase for the mending of the world? That same God who suffered on the cross and goes on suffering with his people. In that moment the silence of prayer meets the prayer of silence.

The experiences at Mount Sinai, which are largely about God being inaccessible and transcendent, came together in a different way on the Mount of Transfiguration (Matt. 17.1–13; Mark 9.2–10; Luke 9.28–36). Here God is experienced in an immanent and local way with great clarity and lucidity. By tradition, though again this is contested, the event happened on Mount Tabor, near to Nazareth. A charming tree-covered domed hill, rising from the plain of Jezreel across from Megiddo, this hill, no doubt because of its breast-like shape, has been given a female image in ancient literature. I recall walking down it one May with every step underfoot squashing an array of wild flowers and the air being filled with the smell of pine, oak and cyprus trees, each offering their unique aromas in the heat of the day.

Luke's Gospel frames the transfiguration story in the context of prayer being the purpose of the mountain climb. This was, of course, the culmination of other journeys in the uplands: Mary had carried the Christ child in her womb across the hill country of Judaea when she visited her relative Elizabeth (Luke 1.39); Jesus, in the hills about the Sea of Galilee, had given his Sermon on the Mount (Matthew 5.1—7.29) with its Beatitudes, metaphors of salt and light, and an expounding of the law, together with reflections about ostentation, judgement and holiness. The Sermon on the Mount is full of hard sayings that were heard in astounded silence; the new Moses was speaking and people responded in a silent pause reminiscent of Elijah's experience of God. Moses and Elijah are drawn into this moment of theophany as Peter, James and John experience their presence alongside a transformed and gleaming Jesus, disclosing his true self to them. From within the Orthodox tradition Vigen Guroian noted, 'For a few precious moments Peter and James and John were also transformed by the light; they were filled with the presence of God and with spiritual eyes saw in Christ the glory of their own transfigured humanity.'[19]

Some scholars suggest that this is in fact a resurrection story that has, through time, become misplaced and been relocated in the middle of the Synoptic Gospels rather than at the end. That misses the point of the story in its location, for I believe it is an event that is preparing the disciples for Jerusalem, in which direction the Gospels now turn, and it is disclosing that this Jesus who is before them comes from the shadow of Moses to become the new lawgiver, and from the shadow of Elijah as the new prophet. The disciples' experience is certainly one of an encounter with the living God in human flesh, so much so that Peter wants to box the moment up and house it artificially for posterity. However, again we discover that God is beyond being packaged into shrines.

When we encounter God in the mountains, when that veil into the unknown lifts for a fleeting moment, we can also have a tendency to want to capture the experience and, by somehow bottling it, keep it for ever or store it as a resource to be drawn on again later. We are caught between experiencing silent awe and wishing to give the moment expression, between simply being present in the embrace of the moment and wanting to make a creative response. Keeping faith with what we have seen demands of us both remembering and rootedness, so that the experience does not leave us so heavenly minded that we are of no earthly use nor sinking into a deep depression amid our everyday experiences.

As if to underline this fact, all three Synoptics have Jesus and the three disciples descend the mountain and immediately face a demanding pastoral encounter that must have earthed this whole mountaintop experience. Jesus meets a man with an epileptic son. We are given the detail that this is his only son, his heir, in a culture where the heir would provide for the father in old age. Here was a situation that would only get worse as the years progressed; a situation that would lead to its own place of Golgotha. Jesus brings the mountaintop experience down into the valley and by healing this boy lifts him and his father up to their own unique experience of mountain glory in their lives.

While Golgotha is not referred to in Scripture as being on a hill, it has assumed this reputation. It was, of course, placed geographically just outside the city walls of Jerusalem, itself built on Mount Zion, and by tradition the Temple was built on Mount Moriah, the place of Abraham's planned sacrifice of Isaac (Gen. 22.2). In iconography the cross is frequently painted with the skull of Adam at its base, which stems from the medieval legend that Golgotha, the place of the skull (Mark 15.22), was the mountain at the earth's centre. Immediately it presents us with a problem about how we describe this place. Often we are drawn to landscapes because of their beauty. The cross, with all its horror, injustice and death, stands counter-cultural to how we perceive a beautiful landscape. So can Golgotha be described as beautiful? The theologian Hans Urs von Balthasar, encountered in Chapter 1, argued that theological aesthetics, beauty, is grounded in God's freely uttered self-revelation in Jesus Christ,[20] and that if Christ is God, then the way of Christ in all its ways is beautiful, including the Passion.[21] So if the Passion is beautiful, as it is a manifestation of God, we are then left to doubt whether what in landscape terms we call beautiful is authentic. Stephen Fields, who advanced this argument, commented:

> Once theological aesthetics takes as its measure the apparent ugliness of the cross, our common understanding of beauty seems to crumble. Once God utters his absolute Word in the freely chosen ignominy of his own death, world aesthetics seems to lose its foundation.[22]

The landscape of the cross makes us look again at places of ugliness, so as to see God already there, delighting in that which we do not see and willing the localities' transformation. Just as the beauty of the cross can only be seen through the transforming prism of the resurrection, so we can begin to see the God-given potential in the ugly, broken and despised places of the world. While we might have the natural temptation to always flee these places, they may have much to reveal to us if only we dare stay awhile. This reminds us that scenic landscapes, which this book largely covers, do not have the monopoly on theophany.

There is a story told that during the First World War a young soldier on the Western Front is said to have turned to a colleague in the hell of the rat-infested muddy trenches, with shells exploding around them and the imminent fear of death filling the darkest places of their minds, and said, 'We were not made for this.' The same is true wherever ugliness keeps the full glory of God in creation from being revealed. When we hear of a victim of genocide or see a homeless person, do we acknowledge that we were not made for this? Likewise the whole created order in landscapes was not made to be squandered, polluted and destroyed.

What unites the mountains of Moriah, Sinai, Tabor and Golgotha is that they are all places of prayer, of revelation and of transformation. At the end of Matthew's Gospel (Matt. 28.16–20) the risen Jesus directs his disciples to meet him on a mountain in Galilee, and there these themes come together. In that moment there is prayer as 'they worshipped him', together with revelation as 'Jesus came' promising to be present until 'the end of the age', and there is transformation, as they are given the commission to be freed to 'make disciples of all nations, baptizing them in the name of the Father and of the Son and of the Holy Spirit'. There, as before, the mountain in a sense becomes the altar on which God's presence is made known.

By going up the mountain, literally and metaphorically, we can leave something of the world behind – perhaps difficulties, tensions or injustices that we face – and become open to the invitation of God. If we reach the summit, in that vastness that lies before us, so God is also present because neither 'height, nor depth, nor anything else in all creation, will be able to separate us from the love of God in Christ Jesus our Lord' (Rom. 8.39). It is then that perhaps we can join with the psalmist in saying, 'I lift up my eyes to the hills' (Ps. 121.1), knowing that that is from where our help comes.

6

Desert

A bumpy taxi ride from Bethlehem took me past olive trees growing on stony terraces, where young boys threw stones at their scraggy sheep to keep them in the shade. Beyond the municipal rubbish tip smouldering in the sun, a modern Gehenna whose stench stuck in the nostrils for most of the day, the stones became more abundant and the valley sides more sheer as the vegetation disappeared. Two rectangular Byzantine watchtowers, peeping up in the harsh barren hills of the Judaean desert, gave the only clue to the ancient monastery of Mar Saba perched on the side of the canyon-like Kidron valley. Reputedly the oldest inhabited monastery in the world, founded in 483, this Eastern Orthodox community houses about 20 monks living an austere life of prayer and study in their buttressed network of terraces and cupolas within the huge fortified walls of their enclosure. William Dalrymple, in his book *From the Holy Mountain*, summed the place up by suggesting:

> despite its rocky solidity, the monastery's implausible position on a cliff-face in the midst of the wilderness somehow gives the place a fantastic, almost visionary appearance,

like one of those castles in children's fairy tales capable of vanishing in the blink of an eye.[1]

Down the centuries this place has attracted men who have searched out the space and openness of the desert. The face of the pitted, honeycomb cliff across the valley tells countless stories of monks who took themselves off for periods in order to experience the wilderness more intensely, living in individual cells yet within sight of the mother-house.

As we explore the Scriptures so we find characters who went out into the desert in search of isolation. We hear of wanderings through the wilderness as Moses led the Israelites from their bonded lifestyle in Egypt to within sight of freedom in their Promised Land of milk and honey in Canaan. This desert experience was to shape them as a people more than anything else. We also encounter stories that unfold in the Judaean desert or Negeb, south of the Promised Land. These are dry, parched places, with scattered nomadic communities eking out a livelihood. When it does rain the water can run off the land so quickly that the wadis flood, scouring everything in the path of the surge of water.

In general the biblical writers are fairly negative about the wilderness desert: 'The great and terrible wilderness, an arid waste-land with poisonous snakes and scorpions' (Deut. 8.15); 'a howling wilderness waste' (Deut. 32.10); 'a parched land' (Hosea 2.3); and a 'land ruined and laid waste' (Jer. 9.12). Jeremiah calls it a landscape 'not sown' because it is beyond cultivation (Jer. 2.2). Running out of water and food was a perpetual concern, that meant almost certain death. Add to these difficulties outlaws, and fugitives escaping the law, and the desert landscape gained a cut-throat and dangerous image. Then there were wild animals such as lions, asses and jackals; some of whom the Bible carries an ambiguity about, whether they have a supernatural quality. The desert conveys a sense of great foreboding. It was seen as being outside normal society, a place with none of life's props and resources, a landscape of desolation and death, and a symbol of God's absence. Liturgically this was lived out each year on the Day of Atonement, when two goats were prepared. One was sacrificed; the other, the scapegoat, had the sins of the whole people placed upon it and was then taken out and released in the wilderness desert (Lev. 16.10).

About to leave his home and his settled existence, to move from Ur and travel into this desert wilderness, was Abraham. His name means literally 'father of the multitude' and he saw himself as a shepherd. The details about why he decided to leave are lost in history. Perhaps he was disillusioned by civilization, or concerned that his people were losing touch with precious things from their culture and history, or perhaps it was an environmental concern such as a shortage of food. It is in the desert that the new nation begins its formation, and later will be reshaped, during the exodus. The desert will also form the location for other aspects of the story associated with Abraham, particularly the story of Hagar; a story of human complexity and one that no one comes out of very well.

Hagar was a slave-girl in the household of Abraham and Sarah. This was a home that had received a promise that Abraham would be the father of a great dynasty. The problem was that no child had arrived, and Abraham and his wife became increasingly desperate as the years went by. What was this of God, not to keep a promise? So the couple take things into their own hands and agree to use a surrogate mother. Hagar is used for this purpose. All appears to be going well, with a healthy pregnancy. Then the jealousy begins, with Sarah feeling that Hagar is looking down on her; Abraham, seemingly exasperated with the situation, says to Sarah, 'Do to her as you please' (Gen. 16.6). Having been dealt with harshly, Hagar runs away into the desert.

It is in that wilderness place, not knowing where to go next, with her life in disarray and carrying her master's child, that an angel of the Lord meets her and tells her to return. She gives the Lord a new name, El-roi, meaning 'God of seeing', and names her son Ishmael.

However, this does not stop the jealousy. With the eventual arrival of Sarah's own son, Isaac, and on the day of celebration to mark his weaning, Sarah sees Ishmael and Isaac playing together, and she cannot bear it. Paranoid about the role each will play in the future, and who will be the heir, she encourages Abraham to cast out Hagar and Ishmael. It's a dark moment for Abraham. Reluctantly he sends Hagar and their son out into the desert with meagre provisions. Their water runs out and all seems lost. Ishmael is placed under a bush, which affords him a little comfort in the shade, as the inevitable slow death from dehydration brings a haze across the scene. His mother, too frightened to watch, sits a distance away, awaiting her own demise. The whole scene is pitiful and distressing. There is a silent waiting. The story recounts how again God sees the situation and provides for their needs, supplying a well in the wilderness. Ishmael was to grow up in that place, becoming a proficient hunter – he was 'an expert with the bow' – before his mother 'got a wife for him from the land of Egypt' (Gen. 21.20–21). So the angel's prophecy that Ishmael would be a 'wild ass of a man', in other words a desert-dweller, comes true, and the harsh environment of the desert proves the depth of God's love.

There are many parallels between this story and the wider story of the exodus of the Israelites from slavery in Egypt years later. The Israelites were slaves, just as Hagar was. As the Israelites became a threat to the Pharaoh, growing in number, so also Hagar became a threat to Sarah when she conceived and later gave birth to a son. The Israelites escaped, just as Hagar did from the cruelty of her mistress. Moses and Hagar both meet

God in the desert at their lowest moment and in their greatest need for survival. It is in the desert, to where Hagar is finally exiled, that, like the Israelites in the wilderness and later in their Babylonian exile, she faces her most agonizing and purifying time. This goes to the heart of the pain in the story. She is the one who has been at the whim of Sarah's paranoia and Abraham's weakness, and in the end is left excluded. As such she is an icon for all those who get pushed into the deserts of the world, both metaphorically and physically.

Tragically, there are countless examples of the poor being pushed to the margins: to the arid places of the world to sift sand for food. We see the poor scavenging in bins behind restaurants in London. In Ghana, to the west of the capital Accra, the poor try to survive amid the toxic heaps of the city's rubbish. We see Hagar also in the face of the individual cast out by family, or community, or country. Her face appears in those more hidden deserts of our own mind: the places where loneliness shivers and friends run a mile, where we feel hopeless and lost with no sense of future direction. What this story tells us is that while the desert is a fearsome place, it is also a place of meeting, transition and change; God does not abandon us in the wilderness. Rather God is a God of embrace, of loving mercy, of reconciliation, of healing and wholeness, always longing that all might in the end come to blossom in the desert.

This was certainly true for the Israelite people. They left Egyptian control as slaves, and some 40 years later, in an exercise of radical faith, were transformed into a disciplined nation. In the desert they discovered the faithfulness of God's love and God's deep longing for their faithfulness in return. It was there that God was revealed to Moses and the Israelites through the experience of the burning bush, the pillars of cloud and fire, and in the giving of the law on Mount Sinai. In the desert the people are transformed by God's presence and self-revelation into a new beginning. It is the crucible in which their identity is shaped. The desert, Herbert Schneidau has commented, was the fitting place for God's revelation to Moses because 'the unearthly landscape of the desert is not God's "home" but a scene appropriate to him, for he too is unearthly'.[2] Through the removal of the usual props on which they relied they were tested as a people by the God who was being made known to them and was concerned about how they would keep his commandments. In the wilderness of Zin these thirsty people complain bitterly to Moses: 'Why have you brought us up out of Egypt, to bring us to this wretched place? It is no place for grain, or figs, or vines, or pomegranates; and there is no water to drink' (Num. 20.5; the story is recorded in Deut. 8.15). The potential mutiny is averted as, following the prayers of Moses and Aaron, God commands Moses to hit his staff against a rock and a spring appears.

This wilderness rite of passage clarified their faith and belief and turned the people back to rely upon God and not on false hopes or the idolatry of a golden image. The story seeped into the imagination, the psalmist recalling, 'O God, when you went out before your people, when you marched through the wilderness . . . rain in abundance, O God, you showered abroad; you restored your heritage when it languished' (Ps. 68.7, 9). Belden Lane noted that, 'They cover gruelling miles of terrain so tortuous they will never be tempted to re-cross it in quest of the leeks and onions they remembered in Egypt.'[3] Walter Brueggemann summed up the historic episode: 'Wilderness should have been a place of death, but life is given. Wilderness should have been a place of weariness, sickness, poverty and disease, but Israel is sustained and kept well.'[4] At times it would come to be regarded as an idealized time, Jeremiah speaking of those days as a youthful devotion (Jer. 2.2), which were followed by a period of disobedience as Israel forgot her past and what God had provided for her.

We see the theme of the desert re-emerging in the sixth century BCE when the Jews of the kingdom of Judah were in exile in Babylon. Isaiah makes prophetic promises that there will be a second exodus, speaking of hills and valleys being flattened (Isa. 40.3–4), rivers flowing in the desert (Isa. 35.6 and 43.19–20), and the desert rejoicing and full of colour: 'like the crocus it shall blossom abundantly, and rejoice with joy and singing' (Isa. 35.1).

Just as the Israelites had come through the waters of the Red Sea into a period of testing, so Jesus comes through the waters of baptism to be driven into the desert, as Mark's Gospel puts it (Mark 1.12), to be tempted about food, safety and power. These were all issues of importance to the exodus generation and, as if to underline this link, Jesus' answers to the devil's enticements are quotations from Deuteronomy's wilderness period. To the call to use his power to turn stones into bread, a few words from a longer verse: '[God] humbled you by letting you hunger, then by feeding you with manna, with which neither you nor your ancestors were acquainted, in order to make you understand that one does not live by bread alone, but by every word that comes from the mouth of the LORD' (Deut. 8.3). In refusing to put God to the test by jumping from the pinnacle of the Temple: 'Do not put the LORD your God to the test, as you tested him at Massah' (Deut. 6.16), which recalls the arguments over water and whether God was with his people in the wilderness. The offer that in return for worshipping the devil, all that Jesus could see would be his, is given a rebuttal that recalls God's faithfulness 'who brought you out of the land of Egypt' (Deut. 6.12), even with echoes of the golden calf incident: 'the LORD your God you shall fear; him you shall serve, and by his name alone you shall swear' (Deut. 6.13). The inference is clear. Jesus comes through this desert period of temptation on a stronger footing than did his forebears, and is ready to fulfil his mission. Like Israel before him, he has to take the difficult desert route; the route of the desert is the route of death which, of course, Jesus is choosing.

All the biblical characters reviewed thus far experienced the desert landscape as both transitory and transitional. Deserts are places, both physically and metaphorically, that St Jerome said 'love to strip bare'.[5] We are stripped bare, like bones left to be bleached white on the desert sand, of all that usually sustains us in such a place, while at the same time being opened up to God's revelation. They are places where it is difficult for us to hide under the mask of our own inventing or the role-play games that we inevitably engender. We are opened to something different. As Michael Ondaatje commented in his novel *The English Patient*, 'A man in a desert can hold absence in his cupped hands knowing that it is something more than water'.[6] This is why St John of the Cross (1542–91), in his spiritual work *Ascent of Mount Carmel*, had a preference for such harsh environments. He recognized various kinds of environment where God could stir the human heart. The first was the attractive scenic and forested landscape, but he warns that such places contain the danger of distraction due to their charm. He felt that the more important landscape was one that was solitary and austere, with no distraction, such as the desert. There the individual is pushed towards the outer regions of human experience and their ego reduced. This was something that Thomas Merton noted when he observed that the Desert Fathers had to 'reject the false, formal self, fabricated under social compulsion in the world'.[7] From a Jewish perspective, Michael Comins, who leads Judaean desert treks, wrote: 'Wilderness matters because it is an optimal environment in which to work out an unmediated, direct relationship with God'.[8]

In the desert, both physical and metaphorical, we can find ourselves struggling with God, with ourselves and with life itself. In the physical desert, if you do not have a respect for the heat, the dryness, the wind, and the distances then they will kill you. Life is never simple in the desert and you have to be attentive to the landscape. In the desert of the soul, all can become dry; like the psalmist, we call, 'O God, you are my God, I seek you, my soul thirsts for you; my flesh faints for you, as in a dry and weary land where there is no water' (Ps. 63.1). The desert can be a place where God can seem hidden and, as Belden Lane has written, 'where love at times seems almost cruel, but it is also the place where deepest intimacy and trust are learned'.[9] As such, deserts plumb the depths of our understanding, where we struggle with our doubts and uncertainties. 'It is often in places of fragility and vulnerability that our journey back to God begins,' John Pritchard, Bishop of Oxford, wrote, 'when everything else is stripped away and it's just you, nature and God, nature may well respond and reveal the secrets of her Creator.'[10]

Old Testament stories point to deserts being places of waiting for a dawning realization to happen, whether that be Abraham's discernment, or Hagar and Ishmael's impending death, or a new beginning for Moses and his people. Deserts ask us to wait and don't give us easy answers to our quest for clarity. Jesus took time out and needed the contemplative life of the desert to fuel his ministry. Frequently he returned to lonely places (see, for example, Mark 1.35; 6.30–32; Luke 5.16; 6.12) to pray, to escape publicity, to rest, to think things through, and to be private in the midst of all of his busyness and the competing demands upon him. Sometimes this was just for a few hours; at other times it lasted for days. Deserts can be places that refuel batteries so that we might go back to give yet more of ourselves in service to others. That is why the practice of a regular retreat is of huge value. A retreat allows us not only the opportunity to rest awhile and to catch up on those much-needed aspects of sleep, rest and exercise, but also that precious 'doodle' time, allowing God to speak to us in ways that we don't often hear from within the frenetic pace of family, work or other commitments. This is a gift of re-treating ourselves to a waiting on God. At first it may seem like being in a wilderness, as we adjust to being away from the smartphone, the TV and the other distractions of the everyday. Slowly the sense can emerge that the retreat is an oasis, a resting at the spring, and the every-day that surrounds us is in fact the wilderness – though we continually kid ourselves that it is not. Even in our daily routine, it is possible to build in a mini-pattern so that we take a few minutes each day, or a few hours each week, to re-treasure with a greater sense of clarity some of the simpler things in life.

St Paul of Thebes (d. *c.*340) is thought to have been the first Christian monk to pack his bags and set off for a solitary life in the desert, in the third century. According to legend, as a young man he fled the persecutions of Decius and Valerianus around the year 250, and lived in a cave near a spring and a palm tree. The spring provided him with water, the palm tree with clothing and food, and then later in life a raven began to bring him half a loaf of bread each day. This must have been sufficient, as he lived there until his death, at the age of nearly 100, in about 341. His story is said to have inspired St Anthony (*c.*251–356) to develop a pattern of monastic asceticism and solitude in Egypt. Anthony's first sojourn into the desert was to an area called Nitria in modern Libya, where he remained for 13 years. According to St Athanasius of Alexandria (*c.*296–373), the devil fought Anthony with an overpowering sense of laziness and sheer boredom, interspersed with the untouchable excite-ment of phantom women. Anthony was to overcome all these distractions through the power of prayer, but at one point he became unconscious, later recalling that he had been knocked out by the devil in a fight. In that area it was thought that the prayers of the faithful sent evil spirits out of the cities and villagers to dwell in the desert, so the local villagers, possibly feeling some sense of responsibility and guilt, took care of Anthony until he made a full recovery. Then off he went again to the desert, this time to an abandoned fort near the Nile, where he led an enclosed life, his food and water being passed to him through a crevice in the wall. Again plagued by phantoms, this time of dangerous wild animals, he laughed scornfully at them and they melted away. This must have worked, as he lived in the desert there for a further 20 years.

From this early devotion spread a movement of ascetics, hermits, monks and nuns living mainly in the Scetes desert of Egypt. Such were the numbers that Athanasius wrote that 'the desert had become a city'.[11] The desert fathers and mothers, as this group were collectively called, had a major influence on the development of Christianity and from their informal gatherings emerged the model for the Christian monastic way of life. Christianity came to be recognized by, and the official religion of, the Roman empire during the fourth century, and so the risk of martyrdom for professing Jesus Christ was much reduced, and the desert offered a life of austerity and sacrifice, together with solitude. There was also a more practical reason, as Douglas Burton-Christie noted: 'one of the most basic motives for withdrawal into the desert was flight from troubles of various kinds'.[12] This was a time of Roman reform to the agricultural life along Egypt's Nile, bringing in its wake economic despera-tion and tensions between families as the burden of taxation grew. Fleeing to the desert was one of the few options open to people who could not pay their debts or who were refugees from other heavy responsibilities. The desert provided the monks with 'freedom from anxiety about the future; freedom from the tyranny of haunting memories of the past; freedom from an attachment to the ego which precluded intimacy with others and with God', with the hope that this would release them into such positives as 'freedom to love others; freedom to enjoy the presence of God; freedom to live in the innocence of a new paradise'.[13] In the desert their lives were marinated in the Scriptures, with 'certain key texts . . . especially those having to do with renunciation and detachment . . . serving as primary sources of inspiration for the whole movement', so that 'the characteristic spirituality or expression of holiness which emerged in the desert movement was a fundamentally biblical one: the monks appropriated Scripture so deeply that they came to be seen by their contemporaries as living "bearers of the word"'.[14] Curiosity about this life, together with the wisdom and holiness it engendered, drew people seeking advice and counsel to the desert inhabitants. As their reputation for wisdom spread, slowly the literature of the desert mothers and fathers began to be shared, some collected together under the heading of 'sayings' and other elements forming early editions of rules for the monastic way of life. Later this was to influence St Benedict (480–547) and others, as they established monastic communities learning to live humanely together under God.

Yet we should not see this way of life as in any sense isolated, or totally cut off. Despite its geographical isolation Mar Saba, where this chapter opened, was a great centre of learning and scholarship. In one of its cells, St John Damascene (*c*.676–749) wrote his great *Fount of Knowledge*, a great encyclopaedic work of theology not surpassed until St Thomas Aquinas (*c*.1225–74) drew heavily upon it in his own writing. So while monastic communities were often found in desert places they were not unconnected with the world around them. Philip Sheldrake, examining Celtic monasticism,[15] has shown that choices for settlements were often in special 'desert' places on the borderlands of existing social structures and networks. They needed to be located so as to combine seclusion and access, as well as practical factors such as a water supply; with few inland tracks, islands (Lindisfarne, Mont St Michel, and Iona) or headlands (Whitby, Hartlepool, Monkwearmouth, Tynemouth) were ideal locations.

These communities all developed rules of life: anchorages for living and encountering God in such places. Because of the hostile environment around them their very survival depended upon routine and structure, which formed the framework in which to live out the community's accumulated wisdom of living the desert way. This, combined with attentiveness, led to their physical and spiritual survival. In a landscape devoid of images attentiveness to the small things ultimately brings wonder.

7

Garden

Thou lookest up and perfum'st all the air,
Queen of the garden; thou unveil'st thy breast,
And pourest forth unto the parent sun
Thy grateful incense. Noble, beauteous flower,
Fain would I copy thee, unlock thy breast,
Fling wide the portals of my heart, and bless
With od'rous gratitude my Father's love.[1]

So wrote the Victorian S. W. Partridge to begin his poem
'The Rose', one in a collection of 32 poems about plants. Each
one is given a comment on a different moral value, including
charity, purity, peevishness, pride and beauty, that 'might rea-
sonably be imagined to speak in a manner more improving
and Christian'. For the Victorians the herbaceous border was
full to the brim with plants representing these virtues: the white
daisy nodding its head in innocence and modesty; the lily show-
ing purity of heart and life; the red rose representing both

devotion to God and the love that we have for another; the
humanity of the sweet violet; and plain and humble honesty,
the flowers more beautiful after death than when alive. This
Victorian sentimentality spurred much similar writing, including the now famous twee garden sign, 'One is nearer God's heart
in a garden than anywhere else on earth'. These words, which
I've heard some people confuse with being from Scripture, were
written by Dorothy Frances Bloomfield Gurney (1858–1932);
they are part of a longer hymn imagining a garden laid out by
God with clear references to the Easter garden of resurrection
where 'the soul of the world found ease'.

But how is this garden space, where God is somehow
nearer, described? Most writers begin by saying that it is
an enclosed space. The Hebrew word for garden is *gan*, the
root of this word signifying protection, shelter, to be passed
over and survive; 'gardens in the Middle East are private and
secluded, usually surrounded by a wall. Protection is provided
by creating privacy, intimacy, and a separation from the forces
that threaten from the outside.'[2] Whatever their size or style,
our gardens are set within a wider landscape, which is often
seen beyond the boundary hedge, wall, fence, ditch or ha-ha,
giving a kind of uncertain embrace. They are also manipulated
landscapes over which humans struggle to bend and thwart
the forces of nature into a submission that can then be shaped
and moulded through cultivation. It is then that we see the
slow arc of a garden's development, from season to season,
year to year, and decade to decade. Each winter our work dies
back and we hope for the miracle of the spring's new growth.
It all takes patience, as gardening is an art that requires a
commitment to the future, involving the need to develop soil
quality and then to plant, water, feed, prune and eventually to
harvest. There is the old joke about someone complimenting
a gardener about her beautiful garden. 'Isn't it wonderful what
you and God have created together?' 'Ah,' says the gardener in

response, 'you should have seen the state it was in when God had it just to himself.'

The Bible does not mention gardens very frequently, probably because of the domination of the early nomadic life or the focus on growing food (Deut. 11.10; Luke 13.19). Pleasure gardens were a luxury for royalty (2 Kings 25.4; Neh. 3.15; Eccles. 2.4–6; Jer. 39.4; 52.7), who also owned vineyards and vegetable gardens. King Ahab stole land from Naboth to use as the palace vegetable garden (1 Kings 21.1–2); we encounter King Manasseh and his son Amon being buried in their palace gardens (2 Kings 21.17–18, 26; 2 Chron. 33.20); and King Ahasuerus threw a week-long party in his palace garden (Esther 1.5). Never once is the royal garden the site of God's activity.

Stefan Buczacki[3] suggested that the first gardens designed to bring pleasure might have been made up of attractive weeds found among the crops and transplanted to be grown around the home. This is something seen today along the Amazon, where attractive plants from the rainforest have been replanted around people's homes. There is archaeological evidence for gardens being designed in a formal way around Roman villas, as illustrated by the garden discovered at Fishbourne in Sussex, which included space for the growing of vegetables and herbs. Later on the historical timeline, little is known about Anglo-Saxon gardens, leading to the conclusion that perhaps people did not cultivate them. However, Buczacki argued that the settled culture that made the Lindisfarne Gospels and fashioned the goods of the Sutton Hoo ship burial would have 'appreciated the pleasure, beauty and solace of the garden almost as much as the Romans before them or the medieval nobility and clergy later.'[4]

During the medieval period there was a huge flowering in garden development. Favoured by monastic houses, much influenced by what they saw on the continent, gardens became enclosed and were taken into the heart of monastic circulation in the cloister. Here in this sheltered microclimate a wide range of plants and vegetables were grown, including temperature-sensitive species from the continent and herbs for medicinal use. From such places legends emerged about the power of plants. One of the architectural gems of the town of Hildesheim, in Germany's Lower Saxony, is the cathedral church and cloister of St Mary. Climbing up the outside wall of the cathedral's apse is a dog rose reputedly 1,000 years old which symbolizes the prosperity of the city. According to legend, as long as the rose bush flourishes, so will Hildesheim. It even survived the 1945 bombing raids that destroyed large amounts of the city, with new shoots emerging from the rubble.

In Tudor England plants started arriving from the places where adventurers travelled. The potato was introduced from the Andes around 1570. These new arrivals were not all good news as exotic foreign species also carried a new set of pests and diseases. Kitchen gardening prospered through the sixteenth and seventeenth centuries, while the eighteenth century saw the development of heated glasshouses and an increasing fashion for clipped topiary and formality. A major revolution changed this fashion when Lancelot 'Capability' Brown (1716–83) and his contemporaries swept away the formal gardens of the wealthy in favour of the landscaped park. With the use of the ha-ha, the park was drawn up to the front lawn, to give the owner a long, clear landscape view with all the elements of romanticism: cattle or deer safely grazing and a folly or ruin in the distance. Then the nineteenth century saw another change in style, with the use of soft herbaceous plantings. Edwardian Gertrude Jekyll (1843–1932) was instrumental in the development of the Arts and Crafts style. Her visual gem of a small enclosed garden at Lindisfarne Castle was laid out in 1911 for the then owner, Edward Hudson (founder of *Country Life* magazine), and she developed a planting plan that took into account the wind sweeping off the North Sea. Today's National Trust gardeners still follow this plan and maintain a delight of summer colour and scent.

Later the fashion turned to gardens containing shrubs and perennials which involve less work than the herbaceous border and provide year-round interest, rather than offering a riot of colour for just a few summer months. Those living in cities and towns were able, following the Allotment Act of 1877, to lobby to become a tenant allotment holder; this saw a steady rise in popularity, particularly during the 'Dig for Victory' campaign of the Second World War when growing your own vegetables increasingly became a necessity. Recently there has been another surge in interest in allotments due to the desire for organically grown produce and a sense that connecting with the land and growing food is an important part of our well-being, an interest shown by the increased numbers of packets of seed being sold. The growth of suburbia from the end of the nineteenth century also gave each family a small amount of ground, leading to the democratizing of gardening, which until then had been a pastime mainly for the elite. Buczacki estimated that there are between 15 and 20 million gardens in Britain and he quoted a 2003 survey of 1,001 people in which 85 per cent said that they had the use of a garden.[5] Now the fashion is to treat the garden as an extra room – an extension to the home – with all kinds of outdoor DIY projects, and a preponderance of TV programmes to tempt and guide you in creating your unique sense of place.

In ancient Rome the term for the spirit or sense of place was the *genius loci*, which conveys something of the enchantment of a place. This sense of place tends to be stronger either if there is a great personal attachment to it, whereby the story links to one's own life story or that of people you know, or if the place is particularly included in stories of national identity or the work of musicians, poets and painters. Examples might include Edward Elgar's Malvern Hills, William Wordsworth's Lake District, particularly the daffodils at Ullswater, or John Constable's haywain on the River Stour near Flatford Mill in Suffolk. More recently, the designation of places as UNESCO World Heritage Sites, and of specific landscapes as National Parks or Areas of Outstanding National Beauty, has resulted in an increased knowledge and valuing of their unique contribution. Contrast these with locations that appear placeless, such as shopping malls, many suburban housing estates, or increasingly the high streets of our towns and cities, which could all belong almost anywhere.

Gardens can exude a similar sense of place, built around their descriptive identity and people's perceptions of the garden's atmosphere. The garden might be a neat ornamental terrace, a series of garden rooms, the manicured municipal ordering of rows of primulas or tulips, the secret garden, a high-rise window box, or the deliberately constructed wild garden. Among other things, their uses might be for medicine, for growing food, flowers and fruit, for contemplation, for play, or for sport. Other gardens might be made to convey calm or power. Contrast the Japanese Zen garden, with its stones and sand raked into patterns, giving a sense of order and calm, with the majestic grand gardens of Versailles, built as a very public statement about French power and wealth.

Among the emotions that gardens elicit may be delight, tranquillity, peace, relaxation, joy, romance and wonder. This gives them a particular use in therapeutic care. At Headley Court, the Ministry of Defence Rehabilitation Centre, medical evidence has shown that horticulture aids the rehabilitation of service men and women who have been severely injured in combat.[6] Similarly, when I was a part-time chaplain in a prison, I well remember the pride that prisoners had in their garden, which allowed them a calm space in a harsh environment to reflect, work, and see things grow and change. We should not underestimate the power that this can bring to rehabilitation and restoration.

Gardens play an important role in the regeneration of urban areas. The 1980s and 1990s saw the Conservative government's scheme of National Garden Festivals, numbering five in all, which aimed to reclaim large areas of derelict land in our inner cities, their legacy being a mixture of parkland and housing estates. David Brown talked about gardens being created on the edge of modern society as 'asserting value and identity over against an alienating environment'.[7] Some successful regeneration schemes in terms of community cohesion and social pride have been around the development of new housing with small manageable front and back gardens. While there is a debate about how this changes communities, when it replaces Victorian street terraces and their small back yards and service lanes, there is a sense that the introduction of shrubs and other plants softens a previously harsh, grey urban streetscape with softer green tones.

At Holy Trinity in Middlesbrough the Victorian church building was burned down in the 1970s; the nave was left standing, but kept roofless as an open cloister garden. In recent years this has been redeveloped to create something even more beautiful, with a labyrinth, fountain and prayer room. In a community surrounded by waste land and concrete this garden is talked about as a 'haven' and 'paradise'. At different times it reverberates to various human moods; there can be prayerful silence, the enjoyment of conversation over coffee, the laughter of entertainment from the local drama group, or the collective sorrow when it is used as an overflow area for funeral congregations. It is registered with the Quiet Gardens Movement, an organization established in 1992 by Anglican priest Philip Roderick, which has a register of around 300 gardens worldwide that offer a place for quiet reflection and prayer.

Looking around a garden has a certain spontaneity about it. Often there will be the surprise of a new vista or detail, different from what would be so carefully framed for a calendar or postcard. But gardens can sometimes evoke fear and confusion, as we have seen with the landscapes explored in other chapters. The high-hedged maze can turn very quickly from a game to a terrifying search for an exit. The Garden at Gethsemane, as we shall explore, was also a garden of fear: as if Jesus had entered into a maze and was struggling to discern the route. It is to some of the gardens mentioned in the Bible that I now turn.

In the Bible's first pages we encounter how 'the LORD God planted a garden in Eden, in the east' (Gen. 2.8) looking towards the sunrise. The Garden of Eden, as it developed in the imagination of those who passed on the stories that make up Genesis, was an enclosed designed landscape planted with trees, a kind of arboretum that was both pleasant to look at and useful as a food supply. Through it flowed a river that irrigated the garden before dividing into four: the Pishon, Gihon, Tigris and Euphrates. It was not 'heaven'. It was very much an earthly place. Adam's purpose was to 'till' and 'keep' the garden, and God introduced animals and birds before bringing Eve into the story. In Hebrew the word for 'till' is *abad*, with the meaning to serve or to be a servant to, and the word for 'keep' is *shamar*, meaning to guard, protect or watch over. Both words imply a duty of care, and an interconnectedness between humanity and nature. Tilling the garden meant that there was always a job to do and it ensured Adam and Eve's physical survival with food. Keeping it is also about caring for and delighting in the landscape's natural beauty. Picking this up, Achva Stein commented that being in the garden was an aesthetic experience:

> the garden is not just beautiful, or the word *yafe* (beautiful) would have been used to describe it. Instead, the word *nechmad* is used, carrying the meanings of both 'endearing' and 'lovely'. This same term is used in the Ten

Commandments for 'covet'. Thus, not only is the garden beautiful, but so much so that one wants to have it for his own. In other words, the garden is attractive and tempting.[8]

This combines Adam and Eve's vocation. This was a golden age when seemingly the animal and plant kingdoms lived contentedly together and the music of heaven and earth were in harmony. The rules were few, but there was one that was to be kept at all costs. The fruit of the tree of the knowledge of good and evil was strictly off the menu. But Adam and Eve did eat. Sin destroyed all that had been. Then comes the sound of God walking in the garden in the cool of the evening breeze. It was the very time of day that we too might have gone for a stroll to delight in the garden. But there was no one to be seen there, as Adam and Eve were hiding, and in his anger God banished them from the first biblical home.

Much of our human longing and story, and perhaps our enduring love of gardens, are about how we return to this home. It is interesting to note that in the Qur'an, future promise is described as a garden paradise. As in Christianity (Isa. 51.3; Ezek. 36.33–36; 47.1–2; Joel 2.3), there is the longing for a restoration of paradise and the hope that at least something of the paradise lost will one day be regained. The Orthodox theologian Vigen Guroian put it this way: 'Every garden is an image and a sacrament of the One Garden, our lost home of innocence, henceforth our inheritance.'[9]

The Song of Solomon contains a beautiful passage where a young man, as part of the unfolding passionate and erotic love affair between him and his beloved, has 'gone down to his garden, to the beds of spices, to pasture his flock in the gardens, and to gather lilies' (Song of Sol. 6.2). The Song of Solomon, one of the shortest books in the Bible, with only 117 verses, is read each year by Jews on the Sabbath that falls during the intermediate days of Passover, and it is fascinating that its theme of the garden landscape connects with the gardens of betrayal and resurrection that we enter during Holy Week and Easter.

The Garden of Gethsemane is the setting for struggle, tears and betrayal (the name is a conflation, as Matthew 26.36–56 and Mark 14.32–50 describe it as a place called Gethsemane, while John 18.1 talks of a garden but does not name it Gethsemane). Gethsemane, meaning 'the place of the olive press', is powerful at many levels. We encounter Jesus struggling in prayer while his exhausted disciples give in to sleep. His tortured prayer comes to some resolution in his words, 'My Father, if this cannot pass unless I drink it, your will be done' (Matt. 26.42), to be followed soon after by his betrayal and arrest. As it was a garden that Jesus used when he visited Jerusalem, being on the route to and from the Mount of Olives, it was not difficult for Judas to lead people to arrest him there. Jesus was taken from a garden, just as Adam was taken out of Eden, but this time we see the main character walking away from his self for the sake of God, whereas Adam walked away from God for the sake of himself.

The place where they buried Jesus was also in a garden. It was in this garden that Joseph of Arimathea had him buried in a new tomb, having asked the permission of Pilate (John 19.38–42). The whole rite was hurriedly undertaken so as not to defile the Sabbath. John is the only Gospel writer to record that it was a garden, and this may, of course, have been used symbolically by him, so linking to his garden of betrayal. On the third day this became transformed from the Garden of Death into the Garden of the Resurrection. John goes on to describe how on the first day of the week, while it is still early and the sun has not yet risen, Mary Magdalene comes to the tomb and is shocked to see that the stone has been removed. Having fetched Peter and John, they find the tomb to be empty bar the burial cloths. Mary, in a daze of confusion and bewilderment, backs away and seems to bump into a man whom she thinks is the gardener, accusing him of body-snatching. It is only when he names her, going to the heart of her identity, that she realizes that this man is Jesus.

As the whole story of redemption unfolds, the beginning and the ending are placed in a garden. In the Garden of Eden a man meets a woman in garden, and here, in this Garden of Resurrection, a woman meets a man in a garden. The beginning has come to an end, and the end now has its beginning. If Eden had been about a garden in which death waits, this garden is a place of betrayal and death in which life in all its glory waits. The garden is the landscape where death, humanity's continuing nagging fear, is overcome. It represents the inclusion of the whole of creation within the outpouring of Jesus' love towards Mary and his disciples and in that garden we glimpse something of paradise. In Arabic, paradise is the meaning of the word garden.

Of course, the man that Mary bumps into is in every way the gardener. He planted out the Garden of Eden so that there would be a paradise with lush growth amid dry soil, water flowing in the desert, and life in a hostile environment. Then in the Garden of Resurrection that same Jesus, the gentle gardener, has planted out the new paradise of renewed faith amid a bloodstained soil; hope is flowing in the desert of empty emotions, and love has won through in a hostile place. To remind us of this, it is a tradition to plant an Easter garden inside the church, often starting with something bare on Good Friday, just three crosses, stones and earth, that is transformed into something beautiful by Easter Day, with the congregation bringing in their own flowers so as to symbolize paradise restored.

At the end of the Bible, in the last chapter of the book of Revelation (Rev. 22.1–5), there is another meeting in a garden; this time, rather than it being between a man and a woman, it is between God and his bride, the Church. They meet in the new Jerusalem, a garden city filled with trees alongside a river, with the text implying that it is set on a great and high mountain. Just as in the Garden of Eden, there is another arboreal landscape, now set in a city, and just as in Ezekiel's vision, there is a river. This is the dream of John of Patmos, of the hope of paradise restored. Christianity's narrative is that this future hope is brought about by the two gardens, of Gethsemane and resurrection, that are the landscapes at the heart of Jesus' Passion, death and resurrection.

Gardens in the Bible, and later spiritual writings, together with gardening techniques and produce, have been used as a metaphor, parable or allegory to explore the Christian journey and how far we are fed, nurtured and watered along the way. So we find, for example, gardens and plants being used to describe the beauty of a loved one (Song of Sol. 4.12—5.1), the coming divine ruler and his kingdom (Isa. 4.2; 11.1–2; Amos 9.14; Luke 13.18–19), the inclusion of the Gentiles within the new covenant (Rom. 11.17–24), and the marks of being a Christian (Matt. 7.17–20; John 15.2–8; Gal. 5.22). The anchorite and mystic Mother Julian of Norwich (*c.*1342–*c.*1416) received a revelation in which a lord sent off his only servant to work in the garden as 'a Gardener, digging and ditching, toiling and sweating, and turn the earth upsidedown, and seek the deepness, and water the plants in time'. As the revelation progressed the Gardener 'should continue his labour, and make sweet floods to run, and noble and plenteous fruits to spring forth which he should bring before the Lord and serve him therewith to his liking'.[10] Mother Julian lived her life in a small monastic cell and from this 'garden' her ideas developed and grew. In turn they produced sustenance for those who came to her, and those who still read her work, for spiritual guidance.

The metaphor of 'God's garden' is used in the Pará region of Brazil to describe the abundance of provision in the rainforest. Walking through the forest with local people is a culinary experience, as they pick fruits and offer them to you. The Amazonian forest has such varied taste sensations. They range from the sweetness of mangoes (*Mangifera* sp.) and the white flesh around cocoa beans (*Theobroma cacao*), to the lip-numbing jambu (*Spilanthes acmella*), and the vitamin-rich berries of the açai (*Euterpe oleracea*). Even thirst can be quenched by cutting a length of branch from the cipó d'água (*Tetracera willdenowia*) as it leaks drops of clear water from its xylem. In such a place no one need go hungry. Saulo de Barros, the Anglican Bishop of the Amazon, told me that, 'God is the Creator of everything and has given us this garden,' and he saw that part of his ministry was to encourage people to regard the landscape as God's garden: 'Part of our work is to keep this as it is a blessing for everyone.'

Writers' views diverge, between seeing the metaphor of the garden in our lives as solely God's work, humanity's own work, or a partnership between humanity and God together on a journey. The garden metaphor has been used extensively in the life of the Church, no doubt because it relates to many people's everyday experience. So we find such questions as: what sort of soil is our Christian journey taking root in and how nutritious and open is it for growth? How do we care for new plants and bring them on, so as to provide a welcome and an encouragement for people to step out in the faith? There is also the interesting question about what we might wish to do to provide protection against society's equivalents of wind, disease and pests? The questions go on, and relate to weeding, thinning, pruning, about which Jesus spoke (John 15.1–12), and the harvest that we are looking for.

At a deeper level Vigen Guroian, in his books *The Fragrance of God* and *Inheriting Paradise*,[11] used the garden for theological reflection and saw it as a sacramental landscape and a major place of formation on the spiritual journey. 'No earthly garden ever is just an *earthly* garden, for God is in the Garden,' he wrote.[12] Gardening brought Guroian closer to God, and he continually saw symbols of God's presence and inspiration in the beauty of the garden. This left him thankful, and his experience was aided by those twin themes of attentiveness and anchorage explored in the first chapter of this book. Guroian described the garden as a place of sensory delight and a place where childhood memories come rushing back with the sniff of an old rose.[13] It was Martin Luther (1483–1546) who said, ''Tis a magnificent work of God: could a man make but one such rose as this, he would be thought worthy of all honour, but the gifts of God lose their value in our eyes, from their very infinity.'[14]

Nothing gives more delight for a gardener than eating a plate of their own vegetables or giving someone a bunch of their own cut flowers. Yet, as any gardener will say, any success is as much about luck and the weather, both of which lie well beyond their control. Gardening is often a mystery. What all this illustrates is that the garden landscape has the capacity to draw us continually into the mystery that is the Lord. As we enter into that landscape we are brought up short to see our own wanton and selfish abuse of creation, a continued thread running through humanity since the original sin in the story of the Garden of Eden. Yet the garden of the resurrection draws us forward in hope of our resurrection to new life. That is why it is important to dig and turn the soil, plant seeds, take time to smell a fragrant rose, run your hands through a rosemary bush – even delight in the warmth of the compost bin!

8

Sea

Many people have a favourite train journey, and mine traces the coast from Newcastle upon Tyne to Edinburgh. Clinging also to the route of the A1, waving goodbye to cars and lorries as we speed on, we deviate only when a hill prevents our straight course and a contoured arc is needed. The sealed carriage keeps in the stale smells of the latest microwaved delight from the buffet, and one has to imagine the smell of the sea and the noise of the water crashing onto the headland rocks and draining from a pebbled cove. Out to sea the horizon is a dirty curve; my eyes refuse to focus on a crisp line. The lobster pots' fluorescent buoys nod on the incoming tide, stranded like Belisha beacons up to their necks in sea. But if my eyes were able to be implanted with Google Earth then they would zoom in on the strand of seaweed with a million flies dancing over the drying pods of air turning crisp and coloured green-brown in the low sun, or the smile on a child's face as she runs, kite in tow, across the beach.

The angular pile of Bamburgh Castle, seat of power during the centuries when the sea was the highway route, dwarfs the distant cone of Lindisfarne's equivalent. Across the deadly sands saints Aidan and Cuthbert trod. Now the safe route is marked with poles, and a hut on stilts provides refuge from the advancing tides for confused timetable travellers. I recall the visit of the African bishop who was amazed at the changing tides that bring solitude to this part-time island, and saw the parting of the waters as his Red Sea moment.

It's then on into Scotland as we hug the coast. At times the rails seem to death-defy the erosion, as a cove cuts in close while decaying buildings of an industrial past stubbornly refuse to fall. Static caravans, their occupants attracted to the sea air from the suburbs, nestle together as the light dances and dazzles on the water below. A lone oystercatcher struts on orange legs, its matching beak not interested in the mussel beds but instead works a ploughed field for worms. We swoop by the nuclear power station at Torness and I start the mental calculation as to how high a tsunami wave would need to be to knock it out, as happened in Japan on 11 March 2011, following an earthquake, and how by the action of a wave all that I had delighted in would change.

In 2006 I received a surprise phone call asking if I would like Hexham Abbey to host a small stone sculpture of a figure lying cocoon-like in a boat. It had been made in response to another tsunami, the one that caused such devastation on Boxing Day 2004 around the rim of the Indian Ocean. This natural disaster claimed nearly a quarter of a million lives across 14 countries and showed the deadly power of the sea, with waves reaching 30 metres in height. It had left hundreds of thousands of people homeless, their livelihoods destroyed. So began a dialogue with the sculptor, Rosie Musgrave, about all the practicalities of bringing *Tsunami Noni*, as she was called, to Hexham. I saw pictures of the sculpture, and we reflected on the space that she would be placed within and how we might respond liturgically to her presence in the church, but the pictures did not do justice to the reality of this beautiful, though seemingly so fragile, piece of stone. She was welcomed during Choral Evensong on a dark November evening and took up a short Advent and Christmas residence in the middle of the Abbey's north transept.

The opening sentences of Evensong recognize that we are a gathered community, from all places, coming together in that place. 'O Lord, open thou our lips', the cantor sang. Yet *Tsunami Noni*'s lips remained firmly shut, as she continued her sleep while we 'shew forth our praise', praying that God may 'make speed to save us' (BCP). We gathered that night in our ineffectiveness, in our imperfections, in the midst of hassles and filled with daydreams, to be for a while in Christ's presence and in the presence of this new sculpture. It was as if we were a minuscule part of the vast worship of heaven, connected with all who were caught up in the sculpture's pilgrimage and with the stories of the thousands killed in the Boxing Day tsunami.

The psalm was the one for the day which, as so often happens, seemed to speak to the situation. The whole of Psalm 40 depends on the opening verse: 'I waited patiently for the LORD; he inclined to me and heard my cry.' The psalmist's God is one who comes alongside, accompanies and listens amid all our searching questions: the 'why?', 'how?' and 'what?' questions of both everyday life and exceptional disasters. As *Tsunami Noni* lay in her boat, it was as if she was waiting. Yet we are not very good at waiting, and want everything, from a mug of coffee to our internet connection, immediately. Anyone who has been bereaved, or who has faced a testing time in their life, knows that it can take a long while to get back to any sense of normality. The sculpture's silence was troubling for some, as they wanted an answer to these questions and many others. None was forthcoming. One person said, 'In the end I settled for the story told of Celtic saints, washed up on a strange shore. Asked where they had come from they said that they had set out in a rudderless boat, not knowing whither they were to go, trusting only to the love and direction of God.'

That evening, the setting of the Magnificat, Mary's great song of praise, was by Geoffrey Burgon. Its modern musical score begins with strands that seem to be in conflict with and surge against one another, before gradually coalescing into a coherent doxology. The words remind us that we are a community that should be turning the ways of the world upside down. God's community is one that is called to seek out the lost, the least and the lonely, to bind up the broken-hearted, to proclaim release to the captives, so that the lowly may be raised up. The massive public response to disasters achieves some of this for a moment. However, despite the fact that those afflicted by them go on suffering, disasters are very soon out of our sight and out of our mind. The sculpture's presence brought back into our minds the enormity of Boxing Day 2004, and we remembered those we had so quickly forgotten about.

Over the next few weeks, *Tsunami Noni* was touched by children, and hugged and cried over. People felt the incredible smoothness of the stone and sensed that it had an age beyond its years, as if tossed over many decades like a pebble in wind and waves and storms but now resting peaceably. She continued to remind us about the enormous dangers of the sea and its mighty power, as the psalmist reminds us of God's 'wondrous works in the deep. For he commanded and raised the stormy wind, which lifted up the waves of the sea. They mounted up to heaven, they went down to the depths' (Ps. 107.24–26a). From the whirlwind, God asked Job if he had 'entered into the springs of the sea, or walked in the recesses of the deep?' (Job 38.16). One of my childhood memories is being aged about seven and on holiday in Cornwall, and being told that the air sea rescue helicopter that we could see above us was not practising but was trying to find a young boy who had been washed off rocks. It hovered for a long time, but with no luck.

We see the natural power of wave action in the shaping of our coast, and how this can dramatically change following a storm or more gradually over periods of time. Perhaps deep in our memory is the story of the Flood (Gen. 7.11—8.13), with its total destruction of life except for Noah, his family, and the menagerie that he collected together in the Ark. Here is an echo of the primeval scene at the beginning of creation, where the waters covered everything until they receded. Part of our fear of the ocean is a return to this memory and the fact that it could swamp and consume us again.

While the great explorers of the sixteenth and seventeenth centuries changed the shape of the world map with each new adventure, and subsequent cartographers plotted the detail of every coastline, we are still largely ignorant of the oceans' depths. The seas provide food, and from deep beneath them supplies of oil and gas, but the depths remain largely uncharted and their ecosystems unexplored. Worldwide there are only 5,580 areas of protected marine habitat, representing barely 1 per cent of the area of the world's seas and oceans. Like other landscapes covered in this book, they are in danger. The biggest threat to our oceans is global warming, leading to increased sea temperatures and higher sea levels, but we are also killing our oceans through the discharge of materials, overfishing, the introduction of invasive species, and accidents of industrial growth.

Covering 71 per cent of the planet, the seas and oceans maintain a fascination for us; as in other chapters, where we saw attentiveness playing its part, the landscape of the ocean heightens our senses as we hear the waves, notice the rhythm of the tides, smell the spray, or delight in collecting shells along the shore line. For the one-time poet laureate John Masefield (1878–1967), who at 15 went to sea himself, there was a lifelong yearning to be present in the midst of the sea. In his 1902 three-stanza poem 'Sea-Fever' he speaks romantically of its attraction:

Sea

I must go down to the seas again, to the lonely sea
    and the sky,
And all I ask is a tall ship and a star to steer her by,
And the wheel's kick and the wind's song and the
    white sail's shaking,
And a grey mist on the sea's face and a grey dawn
    breaking.

I must go down to the seas again, for the call of
    the running tide
Is a wild call and a clear call that may not be denied;
And all I ask is a windy day with the white clouds
    flying,
And the flung spray and the blown spume, and the
    sea-gulls crying.

I must go down to the seas again, to the vagrant
    gypsy life,
To the gull's way and the whale's way where the
    wind's like a whetted knife;
And all I ask is a merry yarn from a laughing
    fellow-rover,
And quiet sleep and a sweet dream when the long
    trick's over.[1]

The poet heard the call of the sea, beckoning him to go travelling again: a form of wanderlust. Throughout the poem he uses imagery, rhythm and alliteration, with repeated hard-hitting sounds suggesting the slapping of waves against the bow of the boat. He conveys a sense of adventure and freedom at sea and, if read in a metaphorical way, the narrator desires a meaningful life, with his final words being the hope of a good death after a life of fulfilment.

We encounter the metaphor of the sea carrying the deceased to eternity in favoured poems used at funerals. One attributed to Charles Brent (1862–1926), a Bishop of the Philippines, is about watching a sailing ship until she fades on the horizon and we say, 'she is gone', and at the same time, on a distant shore, another voice says, 'there she comes', as she appears there. Like the horizon, the sand bar is also used as a metaphor to describe the barrier between life and death. In a poem by Alfred Tennyson (1809–92) entitled 'Crossing the Bar' he sees his own death, which happened three years later, and wants 'no sadness of farewell, when I embark', knowing the pain that this would cause relatives and friends. Instead he hopes to be carried out to the depths of the ocean 'to see my Pilot face to face when I have crost the bar'.[2]

The sea has been used, again like the other landscapes explored in this book, as a metaphor for God. Like God, the sea has a sense of the infinite. It is always the same but is forever new, is deep and mysterious, fearful and wonderful, with a natural pattern of rhythm in the ebb and flow of the tide. Like the talking trees in Chapter 3, some say that the noise of the waves gives them a sense of the divine in conversation. Others speak about the ocean being calming, relaxing and refreshing. Perhaps this is an echo back to the sea from which, as evolutionary science has shown, life originally came. At a time of exam stress I remember being given a relaxation tape of Pachelbel's Canon in D major, mixed with the sound of waves, and it certainly achieved what it said on the tin. Late at night, the shipping forecast on BBC Radio 4 tours the coastal waters with the magical names of Forties, Dogger, and German Bight, before offering the sleepy the relaxation of the tune *Sailing By*. Watching the waves or being out on a boat also gives a sense of time having a different quality. The sea can provide silence, or the rhythm of its sound can become like a constant gentle mantra, so enabling the hearer to reflect more deeply. This can result in a greater quality of prayer, as the sea's rhythm enables something of the self-obsession within us, and the noises that we carry, to be jettisoned into the receding water. Might the sea also help us to listen more carefully? Certainly St Cuthbert (d. 687) found it conducive to prayer, and late one night he was seen going 'towards the beach beneath the monastery and out into the sea until he was up to his arms and neck in deep water', where 'the splash of the waves accompanied his vigil throughout the dark hours of the night'.[3]

Seascapes can be moody places, playing a waiting game. Ian McEwan uses this to great effect in his novella *On Chesil Beach*. We find Florence and Edward staying at a hotel near the beach for their wedding night. The hotel garden illustrates the mood, as it is lit with 'an effect heightened by the gray, soft light and a delicate mist drifting in from the sea, whose steady motion of advance and withdrawal made sounds of gentle thunder, then sudden hissing against the pebbles'.[4] Later, on the beach, their relationship unravelled and, in a moment's decision, the future course of their lives forever changed. This moodiness, together with winter harshness, can overpower people. Around the year 1250, in a letter to a friend in St Albans, a monk writes from his cell in Tynemouth monastery about the hardships of living by the coast:

> Day and night, the waves break and roar and undermine the cliff. Thick sea-frets roll in, wrapping everything in gloom. Dim eyes, hoarse voices, sore throats are the consequence. Spring and summer never come here. The north wind is always blowing, and brings with it cold and snow; or storms in which the wind tosses the salt sea foam in masses over our buildings and rains it down within the castle. Shipwrecks are frequent. It is a great pity to see the numbed crew, who no power on earth can save, whose vessel, mast swaying and timbers parted, rushes upon rock or reef. No ring-dove or nightingale is here, only grey birds which nest in the rocks and greedily prey upon the

drowned, whose screaming cry is a token of the coming storm. . . . See to it dear brother, that you do not come to this comfortless place.[5]

Sailors, who live daily with the potency and danger of the sea, and who know of the times when 'all your waves and your billows have gone over me' (Ps. 42.7), have many tales to tell of the sense of God's presence in times of danger. In support of this they cite Jesus' stilling of the storm on the Sea of Galilee (Matt. 8.23–27) as an assurance of God's special protection at those times when they will also cry out, 'Lord, save us! We are perishing!' They gain comfort from Jesus' presence with his disciples, which turns their boat into an ark of safety. This image of the ark became a metaphor for the Church, described by Cyprian, a third-century Bishop of Carthage, as the 'ark of salvation', and much later inspired William Whiting's hymn, 'Eternal Father, strong to save', with its prayer for 'those in peril on the sea'.

Other stories, such as that of St Paul's shipwreck (Acts 27), also bring confidence. Paul, with others, sailing around the Mediterranean late in the season, is caught, unsurprisingly, in a storm. The crew decide to run before the wind, hoping that the ship would not capsize; then, having taken temporary shelter in the lee of the small island of Cauda, they allow the ship to drift in the face of the full-blown storm. Fourteen days later, despite Paul's dream having given them assurance of their survival, the ship hits a reef and begins to break up. The crew and prisoners, including Paul, swim or cling onto debris and make it ashore on the island of Malta. For other sailors – a superstitious profession – there is the possibility of the protection of Our Lady, Star of the Sea, which is a translation of the ancient title of the Virgin, Stella Maris, or the plethora of saints, including St Nicholas and St Christopher, who have historically offered guidance and a smooth crossing.

Celtic peoples, who used the sea extensively for transport and trade, similarly sought divine assistance to protect them from the power of the sea as they travelled in their small boats. The Carmina Gadelica, a collection of prayers, hymns, blessings and runes, gathered between 1855 and 1910 in Gaelic-speaking areas of Scotland by Alexander Carmichael (1832–1912), includes the Ocean Blessing, which begins:

> O Thou who pervadest the heights,
> Imprint on us Thy gracious blessing,
> Carry us over the surface of the sea,
> Carry us safely to a haven of peace,
> Bless our boatmen and our boat,
> Bless our anchors and our oars,
> Each stay and halyard and traveller,
> Our mainsails to our tall masts
> Keep, O King of the elements, in their place
> That we may return home in peace;
> I myself will sit down at the helm,
> It is God's own Son who will give me guidance,
> As He gave to Columba the mild
> What time he set stay to sails.[6]

For a long time the ocean depths were seen to be not only dangerous but the lair of sea monsters, which caused both harm and deliverance in equal measure; they even reared their heads in the work of the psalmist: 'Yonder is the sea, great and wide, creeping things innumerable are there, living things both small and great. There go the ships, and Leviathan that you formed to sport in it' (Ps. 104.25–26). In the sixth century St Brendan the Navigator (*c.*484–*c.*577) set out on a sea journey with some of his brother monks. One story told by his hagiographer describes them landing on an island that started 'to heave like a wave' when they lit a fire on it. Frightened, they got back into their boat, and the 'island moved across the sea, and when it had gone two miles and more the monks could see their fire burning brightly'. Later Brendan explained what had been revealed to him in a dream: 'It was no island we landed on, but that animal which is the greatest of all creatures that swim in the sea, called Jasconius.'[7] This genre of legend-writing, known as immram, was popular in Irish life between the seventh and ninth centuries; it followed a pattern of adventure, moving by sea from one island to another before returning home, changed by the experience. We see similar accounts attached to the lives of other saints, and in stories from other cultures such as that of Sinbad the Sailor.

A distant echo of this type of narrative is painted on the walls of a small burial chamber in the catacomb of St Sebastian in Rome. There, in faded paintwork, is the story of Jonah and his adventures with a sea creature: evidence that the story was seen by early Christians as a metaphor for the salvation of the Christian through baptism. Jonah was a prophet who had been called to an urban ministry. Instead of going to Nineveh, as instructed, he fled westwards, in the opposite direction, and in order to go as far as possible he boards a ship. God sends mighty winds, and the crew are in fear of their lives; they draw lots to determine who among them is the problem and has caused disfavour with God. Jonah is identified and cast into the sea. He would have been certain to die if the big fish or whale had not somehow 'saved' him. After being in its belly for three days and three nights, Jonah is spewed up on the coast, but not before he has had time to think and come to his senses. He goes on to carry God's message to Nineveh, though when God calls off his threatened destruction of the city, Jonah's prophecy is no longer accurate and he is angry with God. Matthew's Gospel cites Jonah's adventure in the ocean as an image of the resurrection (Matt. 12.39–41): Jonah, trying to run away from God, is brought back to life, through water, after three days.

As we have seen, the sea landscape has the ability to stir one up as well as calm one down. In these places of many moods God is encountered in the ebb and flow of the tide, encouraging a journey that is part of something much bigger that stretches both back before us and forward beyond us. Like Luke's despondent fishermen, out all night on the lake (Luke 5.1–11), we are encouraged to risk the mystery and uncertainty of casting out into deeper water.

9

Sky

It was to the island of Inner Farne, described by the ecclesiastical historian St Bede as 'cut off on the landward side by very deep water and facing, on the other side, out towards the limitless ocean',[1] that the north of England's best-known saint and bishop, Cuthbert, was to take himself. Renowned for his pastoral work, and his outreach to the wider world through his preaching and mission, Cuthbert yearned for a life of solitude. We read in Bede's *Life of Cuthbert* about some of the tension between Cuthbert's desire to enter more deeply into his spiritual life in complete isolation and the demands of his followers, both lay and monastic. Even with the sea barrier, they still flocked to see him 'not just from Lindisfarne but even from the remote parts of Britain, attracted by his reputation for miracles'.[2] Poor man: hounded by the cult of celebrity, even the physical distance could not totally sever his ties. Yet in this location, south of Lindisfarne and in view of the political and royal powerhouse of Bamburgh Castle less than two miles away, Cuthbert was to build himself a turf-and-stone enclosure where 'with only sky to look at, eyes and thoughts might be kept from wandering and inspired to seek for higher things'.[3] It was through his attentive watching of the sky that Cuthbert could find the words and the energy for the rest of his mission.

High above Kielder reservoir in Northumberland, James Turrell (1943–), an American artist and lifelong Quaker, was commissioned to install 'Skyspace', which demands another way of sky-gazing. Turrell is obsessed with an exploration of light, and this is one of a number of similar commissions of his to be found around the world. It can best be described as a circular room, beautifully constructed from local stone, where the artist manipulates our normal perceptions of light and space. During the daytime, illuminated from a circle cut in the ceiling to reveal the sky, it is a contemplative space that draws the viewer to watch the sky and see the clouds scud by. At dusk the colours in the sky-hole become darker shades of blue, then violet and indigo and, as the mood changes, gentle solar-powered lights, charged during daylight, begin to glow in the interior of the space. If it is a clear night you will see the first stars appear, this being one of the darkest night skies in England.

Turrell likes the thing-ness of light itself, so that 'you're actually looking at light rather than looking at something that light illuminated'.[4] 'My work is not so much about my seeing as about your seeing,' he says; 'there is no one between you and your experience.'[5] My own experience of Skyspace brought words from Psalm 19 into focus: 'The heavens are telling the glory of God; and the firmament proclaims his handiwork' (Ps. 19.1), as the sculpture made me look really hard, and in a different way, at the sky.

The sky also featured on the third page of my *Children's Bible*, where there was a painting that has stayed with me from childhood. It depicted a very elderly male figure, with a long white beard, wearing flowing white robes, surfing wonderful cumulus clouds, and about to click his fingers to bring all creation into being. I wonder what damage that picture has done, to more than one generation? When the tooth fairy and Father Christmas were exposed as parental love abounding with joy and pleasure, so this image was interpreted in the minds of many as a figure also resulting from this loving creativity. God simply could no longer be believed in because the image that was spoken about had become unbelievable, or of no relevance, or seen simply as an authoritarian figure bringing fear and dread; he is sitting up there in the sky looking down, watching our every naughty move. For those who hold onto this image, being a Christian becomes about goodness, a desire to please this man in the sky, rather than any sense of holiness.

The history of the God in the sky is an ancient one. In Egyptian mythology the skies were ruled by a god and goddess, Horus and Nut. The Greeks had a treasure trove of sky gods, including Aether, primeval god of the upper air, Chaos, representing the lower atmosphere which surrounded the earth, and Hera, who as well as being queen of heaven was goddess of marriage, women, childbirth, heirs, kings and empires. Rainbows were under the power of Iris, clouds liaised with Nephelai, the clear blue days were down to Theia; Uranus held the rest of the sky, leaving just enough room for Zeus, king of the gods. Roman times were a little simpler, with Caelus being the personification of the sky and Jupiter being the god of the sky and weather. For the Canaanites their god Baal was the rider of the clouds and was thought to reside, when he was not cloud-surfing, on top of Syria's highest mountain holding two clubs, one for lightning and the other for thunder. In fifteenth-century India the mystic poet Kabir (1440–1518) believed that, 'The middle region of the sky, wherein the spirit dwelleth, is radiant with the music of light. There, where the pure and white music blossoms, my Lord takes His delight.'[6]

Across the biblical narrative there are the brush strokes of different skies. The psalmist writes of God: 'You stretch out the heavens like a tent, you set the beams of your chambers on the waters, you make the clouds your chariot, you ride on the wings of the wind, you make the winds your messengers, fire and flame your ministers' (Ps. 104.2b–4). Jesus took note of the sky and used it in his teaching. The well-known saying, 'Red sky at night, shepherds' delight, red sky in the morning, shepherds' warning', comes from Matthew's Gospel (Matt. 16.2–3). Though not included in ancient manuscripts, this saying records how Jesus responded to the Pharisees' demands for a sign from heaven: 'When it is evening, you say, "It will be fair weather, for the sky is red." And in the morning, "It will be stormy today, for the sky is red and threatening."' The point he is making is that the Pharisees use their eyes all of the time for such things as weather-forecasting, but have failed to see the manifestation of God in their very midst.

When we look at a landscape, unless it is either bright and clear or overcast, the view may well include clouds scudding across the sky. Time-lapse photography makes clouds particularly fascinating, and we don't need so much patience to watch them! They move, heaped or layered, tall or short, high or low, wispy or like cotton wool, grey, white or black. Looking closely at clouds reveals all the different morphological types and they tell their own stories as 'cloud colour, shape, structure reveal temperatures, speeds, directions of flowing air, and proportions of water and dust'.[7] They pass in front of the sun, plunging us into shade, and we say that the sun has 'gone in', as if for tea or a bath. I've seen clouds pouring like dry ice over mountain ridges into valleys below, felt the cold air of the sea harr rolling off the Firth of Forth and up through Edinburgh's New Town, delighted in the early summer pastoral scene of a village blanketed in mist, the church spire all that marks its existence, and seen meringue-like clouds hovering over islands. The vegetation on the northern sides of each of the Canary Islands is lush and filled with endemic species because this side is often covered in cloud and has the attendant higher rainfall. The hot south, just a few miles away, attracts the sunbathers and has very different vegetation.

For Michael Mayne, one-time Dean of Westminster Abbey, 'Nothing in nature is more mysterious than clouds, and nothing (to my eye) as beautiful and full of wonder.'[8] They are the drawing board for the imagination, seeing in their formation a person or an animal or other object, or carrying the thought of one being able to sit on them. On a mountain, the cloud that comes down often has a mysterious zone of emerging wisps rather than a sharp edge, leading to a very ethereal and elusive experience. Something of this wonder is expressed by Percy Bysshe Shelley (1792–1822) in his poem 'The Cloud':

> I am the daughter of Earth and Water,
> And the nursling of the Sky;
> I pass through the pores of the ocean and shores;
> I change, but I cannot die,
> For after the rain, when with never a stain
> The pavilion of Heaven is bare,
> And the winds and sunbeams, with their convex
>   gleams
> Build up the blue dome of Air,
> I silently laugh at my own cenotaph
> And out of the caverns of rain,
> Like a child from the womb, like a ghost from
>   the tomb,
> I arise, and unbuild it again.[9]

Our experience of clouds has shaped our language: a state of happiness is referred to as being 'on cloud nine', disappointment is turned around to the optimistic in 'every cloud has a silver lining', and there is the ominous 'cloud of suspicion' and 'dark cloud on the horizon'. Clouds are used to describe a lack of clarity of thinking or reality, in such phrases as 'his mind was clouded', 'she's got her head in the clouds', and 'living in cloud-cuckoo land'; the opposite is described implicitly as the absence of clouds, in the phrases 'blue sky thinking' and 'out of a clear blue sky'.

Artists have chosen clouds to depict the separation of the heavenly and earthly realms; characters sit as if on celestial cloudy furniture above the depravity below. No doubt they were inspired by various biblical stories.

In Exodus (Exod. 19.9, 16) God is met by Moses in a cloud on Mount Sinai which at the same time both reveals and conceals him. This theophany was further explored in Chapter 5, but throughout the wilderness years the divine presence is in the register of a cloud. A cloud is experienced when Aaron speaks to the crowd about their moaning (Exod. 16.10), as a pillar throwing the Egyptian army into chaos (Exod. 14.24), repeatedly on the mountain (Exod. 24.15, 18; 34.5), at the Tent of Meeting (Exod. 40.34–35; Num. 11.25), and as a pillar of cloud leading the Israelites by day across the wilderness desert (Exod. 13.21–22). The divine presence, described as the Glory of the Lord, is experienced years later when a cloud rests on the tabernacle and fills Solomon's newly built Temple in Jerusalem (1 Kings 8.10–11; 2 Chron. 5.13–14). It was so thick that the priests could not go about their work. But cloud also marks God's judgement: Ezekiel sees a cloud departing from the House of the Lord (Ezek. 10.3–4), only to return at a time of restoration (Ezek. 43.4–5).

Clouded landscapes appear throughout Jesus' life. It is from a cloud that God speaks the similar words, 'This is my Son, the Beloved,' at Jesus' baptism (Matt. 3.17; Mark 1.11; Luke 3.22) and his transfiguration (Matt. 17.5; Mark 9.7; Luke 9.35). In a moving coincidence the Feast Day of the Transfiguration, 6 August, is the anniversary of the dropping of the first atomic bomb in 1945. At 0830 local time, the United States bomber *Enola Gay* released its deadly cargo on the Japanese city of Hiroshima, wiping out tens of thousands of people under its deadly mushroom cloud. The atomic bomb was 2,000 times more powerful than any other bomb used in the Second World War, and survivors spoke of it leaving behind a literal and metaphorical darkness over the whole place. This resonates with the time of another death, the crucifixion of Jesus, when there was a darkness that covered the whole land (Matt. 27.45; Mark 15.33; Luke 23.44). It was as if anguish filled the whole sky. The whole of creation mourned his death. The prophet Jeremiah, over six centuries before and in grief for the land so badly managed by its rulers, spoke of the earth mourning as the heavens above grew black (Jer. 4.28).

On the day of the Ascension, with his disciples around him, the risen Jesus disappears when 'a cloud took him out of their sight' (Acts 1.9). This disappearing heavenward has clear visual references back to the story of Elijah, who is also taken up into heaven, although in a whirlwind with chariot and horses of fire (2 Kings 2.11). The experience must have been confusing and worrying for those standing watching. Their overriding question must have been, where do we go from here? At first they seem to do nothing except look upwards. Two angels ask them, 'Men of Galilee, why do you stand looking up towards heaven?' (Acts 1.11). Like the experience of Peter, James and John at the transfiguration, the disciples want to try to hold onto the moment, but instead they are to get on with their lives and the ministry that Jesus has left with them in his great commission. Our lives can also be punctuated by moments of enchantment; encounters with Jesus at the very centre of our lives, the very heart of reality, which likewise send us out in praise and service.

Television weather forecasting now takes us on a bird's eye tour of the country, looking down on clouds, rain, or brighter places bathed in sunlight. Weather forecasters' charts show us long spaghetti-like isobars running across our screens. The nearer the isobars are together, the worse the weather is likely to be. On 15 October 1987, Michael Fish, that evening's BBC weatherman, famously announced, 'Earlier on today, apparently, a woman rang the BBC and said she heard there was a hurricane on the way; well, if you're watching, don't worry, there isn't.' He did go on to say, 'The weather will become very windy, but most of the strong winds, incidentally, will be down over Spain and across into France.' That was the weather understatement of the century, as during that night wind speeds reached 120 mph, and thousands of trees were flattened and hundreds of buildings damaged across large parts of southern England. My grandfather, who daily tended his barograph, kept the chart that showed the mauve-inked line of pressure nose-diving overnight.

In Scripture we encounter the wind of God as the voice of God's creative power. The Hebrew word *ruah* means wind, breath, spirit, and at the beginning of the creation narrative it infuses order out of chaos (Gen. 1.2), while in the story of Noah it blows over the earth for the waters to subside (Gen. 8.1). It returns in Exodus as the east wind bringing the plague of locusts (Exod. 10.13) and then again to push the sea back so that the Israelites might escape the Egyptian charioteers (Exod. 14.21). At other times it comes as the slight breeze (Ps. 78.39), the storm wind (Isa. 32.2), the whirlwind (2 Kings 2.11), and the scorching wind (Ps. 11.6). The land of Israel had its own prevailing winds, coming from each of the four points of the compass. 'The wind blows to the south, and goes round to the north; round and round goes the wind, and on its circuits the wind returns' (Eccles. 1.6), and 'the north wind produces rain' (Prov. 25.23). We find several references to the power of the wind, its variability and its destructive potential. Of the four winds, the south wind could be hot (Luke 12.55) or gentle (Acts 27.13), and the east wind was fierce (Isa. 27.8; Job 38.24), destroying ships on the high seas (Ps. 48.7; Ezek. 27.26), and scattering people (Job 15.2; 27.21; Jonah 4.8; Jer. 18.17). In the New Testament, the Greek word *pneuma* tends to be used for the image of wind, which 'blows where it chooses' (John 3.8). The Synoptic Gospels tell of how Jesus is able to speak his voice into the storm on the Sea of Galilee and bring peace out of chaos (Matt. 8.23–27; Mark 4.35–41; Luke 8.22–25). According to John of Patmos, that peace will prevail in the end days. In his vision he sees four angels, one at each of the four corners of the earth, holding back the four winds so that no wind would blow on the land or sea or against any tree (Rev. 7.1). In such a situation there would be no isobars, no movement on the barograph, as all is infinitely calm.

St Augustine of Hippo (354–430), in his work *City of God*, spoke of 'the peace of the universe [being] the serenity of order'.[10] While he was referring to the Heavenly City striving for a properly ordered (pre-fall) creation, he envisaged this peace in the proper ordering of society, nature and our souls. This internal ordering of ourselves, a re-creating of how we are in relation to the God in whom we 'live and move and have our being' (Acts 17.28), is both partial and incomplete: a work in progress towards peace.

Peace and calmness form the aura of the observatory that is situated near to James Turrell's Kielder Skyspace. On a clear night you get one of the best night-time views of the stars from there. However, users say that even this location is declining in quality, as the glow of orange light in the south-east from the Newcastle/Gateshead conurbation, nearly 50 miles away, gets brighter each year. Sadly, most people are unable to see a dark, star-filled sky from where they live due to such light pollution, and so miss out on the sense of wonder inspired by looking out at a universe of a hundred billion galaxies, each with a hundred billion stars. In England, between 1993 and 2000, light pollution increased by 24 per cent and the amount of truly dark night sky fell from 15 to 11 per cent.[11] The Campaign for the Protection of Rural England, working with the British Astronomical Association's Campaign for Dark Skies, has run 'star count' weeks where people are asked to count the number of stars that they can see in the constellation of Orion. In 2007, 54 per cent of those who took part could see fewer than ten stars. Four years later this proportion had increased to 59 per cent.[12]

In biblical times stars were the arena of God: a cosmic screen on which messages could be displayed. Genesis tells of the stars serving as lights and also as signs to mark seasons and days and years (Gen. 1.14–15); Abraham looks out into the night sky to see countless stars and is told that as many 'so shall your descendants be' (Gen. 15.5). During the time of the exodus there was a concern that the Israelites might worship the stars and create idols out of them (Deut. 4.19). The psalmist describes feeling very small: 'When I look at your heavens, the work of your fingers, the moon and the stars that you have established; what are human beings that you are mindful of them, mortals that you care for them?' (Ps. 8.3); God 'determines the number of the stars; he gives to all of them their names' (Ps. 147.4). No school nativity play is complete without the star to lead the magi to the stall in Bethlehem (Matt. 2.2, 7, 9–10): a sign written in the heavens. Centuries later, a poem included in the Carmina Gadelica would contain a beautiful verse in which Jesus is referred to as the 'Lightner of the stars':

> Behold the Lightner of the stars
> on the crests of the clouds,
> and the choralists of the sky
> lauding him.[13]

God's revelation within the realm of the sky has also been read into lightning, rainbows, and wonderful weather. There is a danger, though, that needs to be registered. Using the imagery of God being revealed in the weather has the potential to suggest cause and effect – a link between God's anger and natural disasters, thereby assigning guilt to the victims of catastrophic weather events. The people of Carlisle had this to contend with as they recovered in 2007 from flooding of the river Eden through large areas of the city. Their then bishop, Graham Dow, made himself very unpopular when he stated that the flooding in that city and in other parts of the country was God's judgement upon human immorality and greed. The press understandably focused on the immorality. By making such comments the bishop failed to communicate a more subtle and important message: that our way of life, through the burning of fossil fuels, is causing climate change and is resulting in more extreme weather. We will reap what we sow and these catastrophes are indiscriminate in their strike, although it is often the world's poorest people, living on marginal land and in flood plains, who are most affected.

When looked at in the widest perspective, open skies can bring a sense of tranquillity to a landscape. Northumberland National Park is promoted as a place with such a quality. It is interesting to note, within the management of protected landscapes, that in the United States there is a strong emphasis on the spiritual qualities of the landscape, but in the United Kingdom, perhaps because of concern around the sensitivities of such language and the contested images that it might convey, the word 'tranquillity' is more frequently used. Tranquillity is a difficult word to describe, being a subjective experience, and it is more noticeable by its absence. It means different things to different people but it is essentially about what you can see, hear or do. For planners, tranquil landscapes are defined as being 'sufficiently far away from the visual and noise intrusion of development or traffic to be considered unspoilt by urban influences'.[14] For some, it might be the whole of a natural environment, while for others it might be simply a landscape with a sense of stillness, often brought by little or no wind. Thus, threats to tranquillity include new buildings and infrastructure, new roads, heavier traffic, more aircraft flying (military and civilian), increased light pollution from urban areas and smaller scale settlements, and noise pollution from business and small-scale industry. Taking ourselves out of situations with pressing needs of an issue or concern, into a place of tranquillity, can allow the bigger picture to be seen: the blue sky space on which to trace our thoughts.

So as I lie on the warm ground at the Skyspace one Friday evening, waiting and looking up to the sky, the sun sinks, leaving red and pink streaks across the horizon, the light fades and I count the stars slowly coming out. One, two, three. According to Jewish tradition the Sabbath has now begun, and in awe I recall him 'who made the great lights', 'the sun to rule over the day' and 'the moon and stars to rule over the night, for his steadfast love endures for ever' (Ps. 136.7–9).

10

The focus of our gaze

During this exploration of landscapes, we have seen how they are infused with the divine and can be ablaze with God's glory. We witness the unfolding of God in the landscape, and the enfolding of the landscape in God. As such, landscapes are places that can continually inspire and enchant us because within them God can feel close at hand; as close as breathing.

National Parks in the United Kingdom carry the strapline, 'Britain's breathing spaces', resonating, unwittingly no doubt, with the idea taken from the second creation account in Genesis: 'Then the LORD God formed man from the dust of the ground, and breathed into his nostrils the breath of life; and the man became a living being' (Gen. 2.7). All births, whatever form they are, are animated and nurtured by God's breath; as the psalmist writes: 'When you hide your face, they are dismayed; when you take away their breath, they die and return to their dust. When you send forth your spirit, they are created; and you renew the face of the ground' (Ps. 104.29–30). God's breath gives life to Adam; and we see how the risen Jesus appears to the disciples, minus Thomas, in their locked house, and breathes on them (John 20.22). The resurrection experience gives the disciples a new birth, with renewed impetus and hope as Jesus encourages them with the words, 'Peace be with you. As the Father has sent me, so I send you' (John 20.21). These stories were gathered into the thinking of the Victorian hymn-writer Edwin Hatch, when he penned the hymn, 'Breathe on me, breath of God, fill me with life anew, that I may love what Thou dost love, and do what Thou wouldst do.' The hymn fights against any temptation for dualism between earth and heaven, noting that by breathing upon us Christ has drawn near and now transcends everything.

The English priest and poet Thomas Traherne (*c.*1637–74) toyed with the idea of the created world, transcended by God, making God manifest. He wrote, 'Of hills and mountains, rain and hail, and snow, clouds, meteors etc. how apparently the Wisdom, and Goodness, and Power of God do shine in these',[1] and he noted the natural elements of the weather as 'God is in all these visibly to be Seen and reverently to be Adored.'[2] Elsewhere he described nothing being more enchanting than waking each morning as if you were in heaven in your Father's palace:

> You never enjoy the world aright, till the sea itself floweth in your veins, till you are clothed with the heavens, and crowned with the stars: and perceive yourself to be sole heir of the whole world, and more than so, because men are in it who are every one sole heirs as well as you. Till you can sing and rejoice and delight in God, as misers do in gold, and kings in sceptres, you never enjoy the world. Till your spirit filleth the whole world, and the stars are your jewels; till you are as familiar with the ways of God in all Ages as with your walk and table.[3]

For this to begin to happen we need to imagine God as both almighty, ruling over everything, and at the same time infusing, sustaining and renewing his creation. This transcendent God is always willing to be immanently known. Looking in this way, we begin to see the intrinsic value of everything and that we as humans are just a part of a whole web of interconnections in an enchanted world. The Benedicite Omnia Opera, or Song of Creation, traditionally sung at Mattins in Anglican liturgy, conveys a sense of the relationship of all creation's praise. This canticle of gratitude and wonder, with its words drawn from an addition to the book of Daniel found in the apocrypha (the Song of the Three) and images taken from Psalm 150, is being lost from the collective treasure trove of Anglican identity because of the move to Holy Communion being the principal Sunday service. While touring the landscape giving praise to God, we are reminded that humanity is merely a part of a much wider chorus of thanksgiving:

> O let the earth bless the Lord:
> bless the Lord you mountains and hills;
> bless the Lord all that grows in the ground:
> sing his praise and exalt him for ever.
> Bless the Lord you springs:
> bless the Lord you seas and rivers;
> bless the Lord you whales and all that swim
>   in the waters:
> sing his praise and exalt him for ever.
> Bless the Lord all birds of the air:
> bless the Lord you beasts and cattle;
> bless the Lord all people on earth:
> sing his praise and exalt him for ever.

There is a tendency, however, to read into this canticle the picturesque and attractive. That is a danger that applies to all the landscapes covered in this book. While they can all be immediately enchanting, their wild, untamed side can be danger-ous, destructive and devastating, and yet God is not absent. Some landscapes can be fearful or ugly, or far removed from the natural world, yet they too are infused with God's presence (even if that is God's presence of sorrow and shame). The term 'a God-forsaken place' can never hold true. Instead we might need to look slightly differently or wait that little while longer, and so become attuned to encounter God's shadow in unexpected and surprising ways. But then that is true of any landscape.

Sometimes our everyday landscape may be that of a city where there is little greenery and the space is marked out by concrete and tarmac, flyovers and houses. We discover, in glimpses of nature, or the care taken by planners to design urban space, that there are the signs of God's presence. Judith Tarren, a former churchwarden who lives in Middlesbrough, recognized this in her local neighbourhood and wrote to me:

> Although the landscape where I walk the dog is not the most inspiring it reminds me many times of the life of Christ. Sometimes it is very bleak and cold, no one is around and it is a bit like a wilderness. Then there are times when there are lots of people and children on the playing fields, lots of noise and clamour, maybe like when Jesus went out to talk to the people. A few weeks ago the trees were completely bare, reminding me of the crown of thorns, now the green buds are beginning to show through, looking forward with great anticipation for the summer, like looking forward to the joys of Easter.

We find a city at the end of the Bible, in the book of Revelation. This heavenly Jerusalem is described as a garden city where humanity lives beside nature: a river, and trees with healing leaves. In, through and over all of this is the risen Jesus, destined to 'gather up all things in him, things in heaven and things on earth' (Eph. 1.10), including the mountains, forests, deserts, seas, and sky, into a deeper unity for 'in him all things hold together' (Col. 1.17). This cosmic Christ fills the whole universe, heaven and earth, with his presence. John Inge has commented that this presence of 'Christ himself is the reintegration of God's original creation, and in Christ God has restored the sacramental nature of the universe'.[4] Inge was following in the way of thought of St Irenaeus (*c.*130–*c.*200), who imagined the whole cosmos infused with God's Word and Spirit, so being the sacramental embodiment of the invisible God.[5]

Landscape is sanctified by the incarnation and it is Christ that we are bidden to meet, even in part, in the moments of enchantment that we glimpse all around us in the created world. In those moments Christ brings heaven to earth, and earth to heaven. In such a way, captured in different language by William Blake, we come to discover the divine in our imaginative looking:

> To see a World in a Grain of Sand
> And a Heaven in a Wild Flower,
> Hold Infinity in the palm of your hand
> And Eternity in an hour.[6]

The problem is that as soon as we have experienced God in a landscape, it is as if God hides. Like walking towards a mirage, the image plays with us and disappears as we draw near. Any attempt to capture the moment of theophany will elude us. R. S. Thomas described this in a line from his poem 'Pilgrimages': 'Such a fast God, always before us and leaving as we arrive.'[7] Like Peter, James and John on the Mount of Transfiguration, we can only keep the memory; the experience cannot be preserved for ourselves or others later. Our attentiveness in the present becomes an anchorage for the future. Any repeat will be due solely to God's gracious gift and how our future attentiveness is anchored in our memory.

For Peter, fulfilment of his mountaintop experience came only once he had experienced the suffering, death and resurrection of the man who had called him to leave his nets and follow. It was only then that Peter began to make sense of it all within his community. For us, the wonder and enchantment we experience in landscapes also ultimately finds fulfilment as we walk the way of the cross. This walk takes us into the outstretched arms of Christ, drawing us together with the whole of the created order into his loving embrace, and forming us as a new community. That community, for all its faults and failings, is the Church. It is in the midst of that group of seekers, faithfully trying to follow the Lord, that our experience of theophany finds expression and depth through challenge, continuity, connection and community. Without a community this experience is an aesthetic that leads us nowhere, lacking any connection to a greater narrative or a continuous tradition, or the challenge that moves us beyond an experience being 'nice' or emotionally 'moving'.

Into that community's celebrations we bring the experiences and memories of the landscapes where we have known God's presence, come within his shadow, or sensed that we have missed him by a hair's breadth. From those landscapes the community gathers grain and grapes, bringing them together in its eucharistic thanksgiving in bread and wine. These ordinary things are *taken*, *blessed*, *broken* and *given* for the life of the whole people of God. Also, into our thanksgiving is *taken* our attentiveness to God in the landscapes we encounter, both the beautiful and the ugly, and the anchorage of their story. The landscapes where we have experienced the God of wonder are drawn in to be *blessed* in this thanksgiving as the arenas of theophany: places where God has already blessed us. But we also draw in those *broken* landscapes that have been overtaken by human greed or sin, looking for their re-creation and restoration at the dawn of a new day, but also for the story that they tell us. Finally, the Eucharist is an ingathering so that we might be sent out, together with the whole of creation, having recognized once more Christ's *given* presence. We leave in order to be ready to encounter him again. We do so both alone and also through drawing others with us, into the ordinary places of the everyday and the surprising moments that we least expect.

There, at the point of our gaze, Christ is already waiting to enchant us. God's sacramental gift is the hope and destination of our longing; a vision of what one day we will be more deeply enfolded within.

Notes

————•◆•————

Introduction

1 <http://www.nationaltrust.org.uk/main/> accessed 17 May 2011.
2 Pritchard, J. (2011) *God Lost and Found*, London, SPCK, p. 88.
3 Hay, D. and Hunt, K. (2000) *Understanding the Spirituality of People who don't go to Church, Final Report*, Nottingham, Adult Spirituality Project at Nottingham University.
4 Inge, J. (2003) *A Christian Theology of Place*, Aldershot, Ashgate, p. 72.
5 Hine, S. K. (1953) *How Great Thou Art*, copyright © The Stuart Hine Trust/Kingsway Communications Ltd.
6 Clark, K. (1949) *Landscape into Art*, London, John Murray, p. 2.
7 Oelschlaeger, M. (1991) *The Idea of Wilderness from Prehistory to the Age of Ecology*, New Haven and London, Yale University Press, p. 42.
8 Oelschlaeger, *The Idea of Wilderness*, p. 45.

1 The contours of landscape

1 Williams, D. C. (2002) *God's Wilds: John Muir's Vision of Nature*, College Station, Texas A & M University Press, p. 8.
2 Oelschlaeger, M. (1991) *The Idea of Wilderness from Prehistory to the Age of Ecology*, New Haven and London, Yale University Press, p. 177.
3 Williams, *God's Wilds*, p. 43.
4 Badè, W. F. (1924) *The Life and Letters of John Muir*, Vol. 1, Boston and New York, Houghton Mifflin Company, p. 209.
5 Brown, D. (2004) *God and Enchantment of Place*, Oxford, Oxford University Press, p. 121.
6 Muir, J. (1992) 'The Yosemite', in *John Muir: The Eight Wilderness Discovery Books*, London, Diadem Books, p. 714.
7 Trevelyan, G. M. (1929) *Must England's Beauty Perish? A Plea on Behalf of the National Trust for Places of Historic Interest or Natural Beauty*, London, Faber and Gwyer, p. 19.

8 Schama, S. (1995) *Landscape and Memory*, New York, Knopf, p. 7.

9 Hoskins, W. G. (1955) *The Making of the English Landscape*, London, Penguin.

10 Pryor, F. (2011) *The Making of the British Landscape*, London, Penguin.

11 Thomas, R. S. (2001) 'The Bright Field', in *Collected Poems 1945–1990*, London, Phoenix Press, p. 302.

12 Jacobson, H. (2010) *The Finkler Question*, London, Bloomsbury, p. 205.

13 Garcia-Rivera, A., Graves, M. and Neumann, C. (2009) 'Beauty in the Living World', *Zygon* 44(2), pp. 243–63.

14 Hopkins, G. M. (1986) 'The Leaden Echo and the Golden Echo', in *Gerard Manley Hopkins: The Major Works*, ed. C. Phillips, Oxford, Oxford University Press, p. 12.

15 Lewis, C. S. (2001) 'The Weight of Glory', in *The Weight of Glory and Other Addresses*, New York, HarperCollins, pp. 42–3.

16 Berdyaev, N. (1949) *The Divine and the Human*, London, Geoffrey Bles, p. 139.

17 Balthasar, H. U. von (1982) *The Glory of the Lord: A Theological Aesthetics, Vol. 1: Seeing the Form*, ed. J. Fession and J. Riches, trans. E. Leiva-Merikakis, London, T. & T. Clark, p. 18.

18 Hopkins, G. M. (1986) 'Pied Beauty', in *Gerard Manley Hopkins: The Major Works*, ed. C. Phillips, Oxford, Oxford University Press, pp. 132–3.

19 Vatican Council II: The Conciliar and Post Conciliar Documents (1988) *Dei Verbum: The Dogmatic Constitution on Divine Revelation*, Collegeville, paragraph 3.

20 Edwards, J. (1778) *An Essay on the Nature of True Virtue*, London, pp. 38–9.

21 Eliot, T. S. (1971) 'Burnt Norton', in *Four Quartets*, New York, Harcourt, Brace and World, p. 15.

22 Brown, *God and Enchantment of Place*, p. 96.

23 Brown, *God and Enchantment of Place*, p. 96.

24 Lane, B. C. (1988) *Landscapes of the Sacred: Geography and Narrative in American Spirituality*, New York, Paulist Press, p. 16.

25 Sheldrake, P. (1995) *Living Between Worlds: Place and Journey in Celtic Spirituality*, London, Darton, Longman and Todd, p. 30.

26 Lees, C. A. and Overing, G. R. (2006) 'Anglo-Saxon Horizons: Places of the Mind in the Northumbrian Landscape', in C. A. Lees and G. R. Overing (eds) *A Place to Believe In: Locating Medieval Landscapes*, Pennsylvania, Pennsylvania State University Press, p. 15.

27 Mayne, M. (1995) *This Sunrise of Wonder: Letters for the Journey*, London, HarperCollins, p. 41.

28 Lane, B. C. (2007) *The Solace of Fierce Landscapes: Exploring Desert and Mountain Spirituality*, Oxford, Oxford University Press, p. 100.

29 Thoreau, H. D. (2004) *Walden, 150th Anniversary Edition*, ed. J. Lyndon Shanley, Princeton and Oxford, Princeton University Press, pp. 90–1.

30 Thoreau, *Walden*, pp. 317–18.

31 Mayne, *This Sunrise of Wonder*, p. 41.

32 Brueggemann, W. (2002) *The Land: Place as Gift, Promise, and Challenge in Biblical Faith*, Minneapolis, Fortress Press, p. 4.

33 Schama, *Landscape and Memory*, p. 14.

34 Habgood, J. (2002) *The Concept of Nature*, London, Darton, Longman and Todd, p. 61.

35 Dimbleby, D. (2005) *A Picture of Britain*, London, Tate Publishing, p. 9.

36 Riding, C. (2005) 'Land of the Mountain and the Flood', in Dimbleby, *A Picture of Britain*, p. 93.

37 Blench, B. (2007) *Jolomo Biopic: Painter, Preacher, Philanthropist* <http://www.jolomo.com/jolomo/biopic.html> accessed 23 May 2011.

38 Brown, *God and Enchantment of Place*, p. 152.

39 Ashley, P. (2007) 'Toward an Understanding and Definition of Wilderness Spirituality', *Australian Geographer*, 38(1), pp. 53–69.

40 Habgood, J. (1997) *Faith and Uncertainty*, London, Darton, Longman and Todd, p. 57.

41 Schmemann, A. (1966) *The World as Sacrament*, London, Darton, Longman and Todd, p. 14.

42 Lane, *Landscapes of the Sacred*, p. 191.

43 Habgood, *The Concept of Nature*, p. 169.

44 Brown, *God and Enchantment of Place*, p. 81.

45 Beckett, R. B. (ed.) (1970) *John Constable Discourses*, Ipswich, Suffolk Records Society, pp. 52–3.

46 Brown, D. (2009) 'Science and Religion in Nineteenth and Twentieth-Century Landscape Art', in S. C. Barton and D. Wilkinson (eds) *Reading Genesis after Darwin*, Oxford, Oxford University Press, p. 112.

47 Brown, 'Science and Religion', p. 112.

48 Büttner, N. (2006) *Landscape Painting: A History*, New York, Abbeville Press Publishers, pp. 283–5.

49 Merton, T. (2000) 'A Life Free from Care', in *Thomas Merton: Essential Writings*, ed. C. M. Bochen, New York, Orbis Books, p. 70.

2 Land

1 Causey, A. (1990) 'Environmental Sculptures', in T. Friedman and A. Goldsworthy, *Hand to Earth: Andy Goldsworthy Sculpture 1976–90*, Leeds, Henry Moore Centre, p. 127.

2 Sooke, A. (2007) 'He's Got the Whole World in his Hands', *Daily Telegraph*, 24 March.

3 Natural England (2009) *Experiencing Landscapes: Capturing the Cultural Services and Experiential Qualities of Landscape*, Peterborough, Natural England; Frey, N. L. (1998) *Pilgrim Stories: On and Off the Road to Santiago*, Berkeley, University of California Press.

4 Mabey, R. (1987) 'Introduction', in Gilbert White, *The Natural History of Selborne*, London, Penguin Classics, p. xi.

5 The Archbishops' Council (2006) *Common Worship: Times and Seasons*, London, Church House Publishing, p. 230; The Archbishops' Council (2000) *Common Worship: Pastoral Services*, London, Church House Publishing, p. 269.

6 Morell, V. (1999) 'Restoring Madagascar', *National Geographic*, February, p. 63.

7 Uhlein, G. (1983) *Meditations with Hildegard of Bingen*, Sante Fe, Bear and Company, p. 88.

8 Chief Seattle (1976) *Chief Seattle's Testimony*, London, Pax Christi, p. 4.
9 Chief Seattle, *Chief Seattle's Testimony*, p. 15.
10 Brueggemann, W. (2002) *The Land: Place as Gift, Promise, and Challenge in Biblical Faith*, Minneapolis, Fortress Press, p. 44.
11 Brueggemann, *The Land*, p. 55.
12 Brueggemann, *The Land*, p. 59.
13 Brueggemann, *The Land*, p. 12.
14 Sheldrake, P. (1995) *Living Between Worlds: Place and Journey in Celtic Spirituality*, London, Darton, Longman and Todd, p. 31.
15 Sheldrake, *Living Between Worlds*, p. 31.
16 Lane, B. C. (2007) *The Solace of Fierce Landscapes: Exploring Desert and Mountain Spirituality*, Oxford, Oxford University Press, p. 46.
17 Lane, *The Solace of Fierce Landscapes*, p. 46.
18 Millennium Ecosystem Assessment (2005) *Ecosystems and Human Well-being: Synthesis*, Washington, DC, Island Press, p. 120.

3 Forest

1 Wainwright, A. (1971) *A Third Lakeland Sketchbook*, Kentmere, Marshall, description of plate 217.
2 Forestry Commission (2010) *2010 Forestry Facts and Figures*, Edinburgh, Forestry Commission, calculated from Table 1.
3 Department for Environment, Food and Rural Affairs (2011) <http://www.defra.gov.uk/news/2011/02/17/futureforestry/> accessed 18 February 2011.
4 Some material in this chapter is adapted from Usher, G. B. (2012) 'The trees of the field shall clap their hands: The metaphor of trees, woods and forests as symbols of creation, justice and hope', in A. Smith and J. Hopkinson (eds) *Faith and the Future of the Countryside*, Norwich, Canterbury Press, pp. 178–200.
5 Stephenson, R. L. (1905) *Essays of Travel*, London, Chatto and Windus, p. 170.
6 Merton, T. (1998) *The Journals of Thomas Merton, Vol. VI, Learning to Love, Exploring Solitude and Freedom*, ed. Christine M. Bochen, San Francisco, HarperCollins, p. 341.

7 Darwin, C. (2003) *Voyage of the Beagle,* London, Penguin, p. 374.

8 Walker-Jones, A. (2009) *The Green Psalter: Resources for an Ecological Spirituality,* Minneapolis, Fortress Press, p. 26.

9 Tabbush, P. M. and O'Brien, L. (2003) *Health and Well-being: Trees, Woodlands and Natural Spaces,* Edinburgh, Forestry Commission; Forestry Commission Scotland (2009) *Woods for Health,* Edinburgh, Forestry Commission.

10 Selman, P. (2003) 'Putting a Value on Woodland: Framework for the Future', *Quarterly Journal of Forestry,* 97(3), pp. 193–8.

11 Henwood, K. and Pidgeon, N. (1998) *The Place of Forestry in Modern Welsh Culture and Life: Report to the Forestry Commission,* Bangor, University of Wales, p. 25.

12 Hamma, R. M. (2002) *Earth's Echo: Sacred Encounters with Nature,* Notre Dame, Sorin Books, p. 85.

13 Bernard of Clairvaux, *Epistola,* CVI section 2.

14 Meyer, M. (trans.) (1992) *The Gospel of Thomas: The Hidden Sayings of Jesus,* HarperCollins, San Francisco, p. 55.

15 Wallace, M. I. (2005) *Finding God in the Singing River,* Minneapolis, Augsburg Fortress, p. 146.

16 Schama, S. (1995) *Landscape and Memory,* London, HarperCollins, pp. 142–53.

17 Bryson, B. (1998) *A Walk in the Woods: Rediscovering America on the Appalachian Trail,* London, Black Swan, p. 61.

18 Hunter, S., Pidgeon, N. and Henwood, K. (2001) 'Forests, people and place: How individuals and communities perceive and relate to trees, woodland and forests in a Welsh context', in L. O'Brien and J. Claridge (eds) *Trees are Company: Social Science Research into Woodlands and the Natural Environment,* Edinburgh, Forestry Commission, p. 19.

19 Chouin, G. (2007) 'Archaeological Perspectives on Sacred Groves in Ghana', in M. J. Sheridan and C. Nyamweru (eds) *African Sacred Groves: Ecological Dynamics and Social Change,* Ohio, Ohio University Press, p. 179.

20 Falconer, J. (1999) 'Non-timber forest products in southern Ghana: traditional and cultural forest values', in D. A. Posey (ed.) *Cultural and Spiritual Values of Biodiversity: A complementary contribution*

to the *Global biodiversity assessment*, United Nations Environment Programme, Kenya, p. 366.

21 National Memorial Arboretum (2010) <http://www.thenma.org. uk/about-us> accessed 10 January 2010.

22 National Trust (2010) <http://www.nationaltrust.org.uk/main/ w-whipsnadetreecathedral> accessed 14 January 2010.

23 MacAskill, E. (2001) 'Family olive groves fall to Israeli attacks', *The Guardian*, 14 April.

24 'Church Resistance goes on after Amazon Activists Die', *Church Times*, 3 June 2011.

25 Ruth de Barros, email to supporters, 26 May 2011.

26 Jones, O. and Cloke, P. (2002) *Tree Cultures: The Place of Trees and Trees in Their Place*, Oxford, Berg, p. 38.

27 Worth, D. (2006) 'Our new cathedrals: Spirituality and old-growth forests in Western Australia', *Journal of Multidisciplinary International Studies*, 3(1), pp. 1–15.

28 Thomas Aquinas, *Summa Theologiae*, 1a47.1.

29 Buber, M. (1970) *I and Thou*, trans. Walter Kaufmann, New York, Charles Scribner's Sons.

30 Walsh, B. J., Karsh, M. B. and Ansell, N. (1994) 'Trees, Forestry, and the Responsiveness of Creation', *Cross Currents*, 44(2), pp. 149–63 <www.crosscurrents.org/trees.htm> accessed 14 January 2010.

31 Austin, R. (1987) *Baptized into Wilderness: A Christian perspective on John Muir*, Atlanta, John Knox Press, p. 29.

32 Thomas, R. S. (2004) 'Tell Us', in *Collected Later Poems 1988–2000*, Tarset, Bloodaxe Books, p. 170.

33 Evelyn, J. (1662) *Silva: or, A discourse of forest-trees and the propagation of timber in his Majesty's Dominions together with an historical account of the sacredness and use of standing groves*, York.

4 River

1 Ransome, A. (1968) *Swallowdale*, Middlesex, Puffin Books, pp. 191–2.

2 Hughes, T. (1969) *Poetry in the Making*, London, Faber, pp. 79–80.

3 The World Conservation Union (IUCN) (1996) *IUCN Red List of threatened Animals*, Switzerland, IUCN, p. Intro-24.

4 Belt, D. (2010) 'Parting the Waters', *National Geographic* <http://ngm.nationalgeographic.com/2010/04/parting-the-waters/belt-text/1> accessed 18 May 2011.

5 Belt, 'Parting the Waters'.

6 Belt, 'Parting the Waters'.

7 See 1 Cor. 2.10 and Eph. 3.18.

8 Mayhew Smith, N. (2011) *Britain's Holiest Places*, Bristol, Lifestyle Press Ltd.

9 Mayhew Smith, *Britain's Holiest Places*, p. 531.

10 Tertullian, *De Baptismo* i.

5 Mountain

1 MacFarlane, R. (2007) *The Wild Places*, London, Granta Books, p. 154.

2 West, T. (1784) *A Guide to the Lakes in Cumberland, Westmorland and Lancashire*, London, p. 12.

3 Wordsworth, W. (1998) *The Prelude*, in *William Wordworth*, ed. S. Logan, London, Everyman Paperbacks, pp. 97–9.

4 Nicolson, M. H. (1997) *Mountain Gloom and Mountain Glory: The Development of the Aesthetics of the Infinite*, Seattle and London, University of Washington Press, p. 393.

5 Bernbaum, E. (1999) 'Mountains: The Heights of Biodiversity', in D. A. Posey (ed.) *Cultural and Spiritual Values of Biodiversity: A Complementary Contribution to the Global Biodiversity Assessment*, Kenya, United Nations Environment Programme, p. 327.

6 Okey, T. (trans.) (2003) *The Little Flowers of Saint Francis*, chapter LIII, New York, Dover Publications, p. 94.

7 Leigh-Mallory, G. H. (1922) 'The Reconnaissance of the Mountain', in C. K. Howard-Bury, *Mount Everest, The Reconnaissance, 1921*, London, Edward Arnold, p. 186.

8 Bernbaum, 'Mountains', p. 330.

9 O'Donaghue, N. (1993) *The Mountain Behind the Mountain: Aspects of the Celtic Tradition*, Edinburgh, T. and T. Clark, pp. 30–31.

10 Shepherd, N. (2008) *The Living Mountain: A Celebration of the Cairngorm Mountains of Scotland*, Edinburgh, Canongate Books, p. 84.

11 Lane, B. C. (2007) *The Solace of Fierce Landscapes: Exploring Desert and Mountain Spirituality*, Oxford, Oxford University Press, p. 40.

12 See Askins, K. (2004) *Visible Communities' Use and Perception of the North York Moors and Peak District National Parks: A Policy guidance Document for the National Park Authorities*, Univerity of Durham; Suckall, N., Fraser, E. D. G., Cooper, T. and Quinn, C. (2009) 'Visitor perceptions of rural landscapes: A case study in the Peak District National Park, England', *Journal of Environmental Management*, 90, pp. 1195–1203.

13 Louv, R. (2010) *Last Child in the Woods: Saving our Children from Nature-deficit Disorder*, London, Atlantic Books.

14 Schama, S. (1995) *Landscape and Memory*, London, HarperCollins, p. 396.

15 Muir, J. (1992) 'The Yosemite', in *John Muir: The Eight Wilderness Discovery Books*, London, Diadem Books, p. 716.

16 Lane, *The Solace of Fierce Landscapes*, p. 137.

17 Wilkinson, J. (trans.) (1971) *Egeria's Travels*, London, SPCK, p. 96.

18 Quoted in Schama, *Landscape and Memory*, p. 414.

19 Guroian, V. (2002) *Inheriting Paradise; Meditations on Gardening*, London, Darton, Longman and Todd, p. 51.

20 Balthasar, H. U. von (1982) *The Glory of the Lord: A Theological Aesthetics, Vol. 1: Seeing the Form*, ed. J. Fession and J. Riches, trans. E. Leiva-Merikakis, London, T. and T. Clark, p. 29.

21 Balthasar, *The Glory of the Lord*, p. 28.

22 Fields, S. (2007) 'The Beauty of the Ugly: Balthasar, the Crucifixion, Analogy and God', *International Journal of Systematic Theology*, 9(2), pp. 172–83, p. 175.

6 Desert

1 Dalrymple, W. (1998) *From the Holy Mountain: A Journey in the Shadow of Byzantium*, London, HarperCollins, p. 288.

2 Schneidau, H. N. (1976) *Sacred Discontent: The Bible and Western Tradition*, Baton Rouge, Louisiana State University Press, p. 142.

3 Lane, B. C. (2007) *The Solace of Fierce Landscapes: Exploring Desert and Mountain Spirituality*, Oxford, Oxford University Press, p. 44.

4 Brueggemann, W. (2002) *The Land: Place as Gift, Promise, and Challenge in Biblical Faith*, Minneapolis, Fortress Press, p. 40.

5 Jerome, Letter XIV to Heliodorus.

6 Ondaatje, M. (1992) *The English Patient*, New York, Vintage Books, p. 155.

7 Merton, T. (1960) *The Wisdom of the Desert*, Tunbridge Wells, Burns and Oates, p. 13.

8 Comins, M. (2006) 'Wilderness Spirituality', *CCAR Journal: A Reform Jewish Quarterly*, Winter.

9 Lane, *The Solace of Fierce Landscapes*, p. 178.

10 Pritchard, J. (2011) *God Lost and Found*, London, SPCK, p. 90.

11 Gregg, R. (1980) *Athanasius: The Life of Anthony and the Letter to Marcellinus*, New York, Paulist Press, p. 43.

12 Burton-Christie, D. (1993) *The Word in the Desert: Scripture and the Quest for Holiness in Early Christian Monasticism*, Oxford, Oxford University Press, p. 41.

13 Burton-Christie, *The Word in the Desert*, p. 222.

14 Burton-Christie, *The Word in the Desert*, p. 4.

15 Sheldrake, P. (1995) *Living Between Worlds*, London, Darton, Longman and Todd, pp. 22–5.

7 Garden

1 Partridge, S. W. (1850) *Voices from the Garden; or The Christian Language of Flowers*, London, Partridge and Co.

2 Stein, A. B. (1990) 'Thoughts Occasioned by the Old Testament', in M. Francis and R. T. Hester Jr (eds) *The Meaning of Gardens*, Massachusetts, MIT Press, p. 38.

3 Buczacki, S. (2007) *Garden Natural History*, London, HarperCollins, p. 1.

4 Buczacki, *Garden Natural History*, pp. 6–7.

5 Buczacki, *Garden Natural History*, p. 25.

6 MOD (2011) Press release, *Growing stronger at Headley Court*, 26 May <http://www.mod.uk/DefenceInternet/DefenceNews/PressCentre/PressReleases/0632011GrowingStrongerAtHeadleyCourt.htm> accessed 4 June 2011.

7 Brown, D. (2004) *God and the Enchantment of Place*, Oxford, Oxford University Press, Oxford, p. 386.

8 Stein, 'Thoughts Occasioned by the Old Testament', p. 43.

9 Guroian, V. (2006) *The Fragrance of God*, Michigan, Eerdmans, p. 49.

10 Mother Julian of Norwich, *The Revelations of Divine Love*, chapter 51.

11 Guroian, *The Fragrance of God*; Guroian, V. (2002) *Inheriting Paradise: Meditations on Gardening*, London, Darton, Longman and Todd.

12 Guroian, *The Fragrance of God*, p. 49.

13 Guroian, *The Fragrance of God*, pp. 5–6.

14 Luther, M. (2003) *Tabletalk*, trans. W. Hazlitt, Ross-shire, Christian Heritage Imprint, saying no. 133, p. 144.

8 Sea

1 Masefield, J. (2005) 'Sea-Fever', in *Sea-Fever: Selected Poems of John Masefield*, ed. Philip W. Errington, Manchester, Carcanet Press, p. 10.

2 Tennyson, Alfred (2000) 'Crossing the Bar', in *Alfred Tennyson: The Major Works*, ed. A. Roberts, Oxford, Oxford University Press, p. 478.

3 Bede, *Life of Cuthbert*, Chapter 10.

4 McEwan, I. (2008) *On Chesil Beach*, London, Vintage Books, p. 5.

5 St Alban's Cathedral MS Ee.4.20.

6 Carmichael, A. (1992) 'The Ocean Blessing', in *Carmina Gadelica*, Edinburgh, Floris Books, p. 120.

7 *The Voyage of St Brendan the Navigator*, Chapter 10.

9 Sky

1 Bede, *Life of Cuthbert*, Chapter 17.

2 Bede, *Life of Cuthbert*, Chapter 22.

3 Bede, *Life of Cuthbert*, Chapter 17.

4 Quoted in an interview with Sue Steward, 'James Tyrrell trips the light fantastic', *London Evening Standard*, 14 October 2010.

5 Quoted at <www.exploratorium.ed/lightandland/turrell-quotes. html> accessed 6 June 2011.

6 Tagore, Rabindranath (trans.) (2008) *Songs of Kabir*, Radford, VA, A & D Publishing, Song XVIII, p. 24.

7 Spirn, A. W. (1998) *The Landscape of Language*, New Haven and London, Yale University Press, p. 142.

8 Mayne, M. (1995) *This Sunrise of Wonder: Letters for the Journey*, London, HarperCollins, p. 147.

9 Shelley, P. B. (2003) 'The Cloud', in *Percy Bysshe Shelley: The Major Works*, ed. Z. Leader and M. O'Neill, Oxford, Oxford University Press, p. 462.

10 Augustine, *City of God* XIX.13.

11 Campaign for the Protection of Rural England (2003) *Night Blight!*

12 <http://www.cpre.org.uk/media-centre/latest-news-releases/item/ 2055-star-count-week-results-a-dark-outlook-for-starry-skies> accessed 3 June 2011.

13 Carmichael, A. (1992) 'The Lightner of the Stars', in *Carmina Gadelica*, Edinburgh, Floris Books, p. 46.

14 CPRE and the Countryside Commission (1995) *Tranquil Areas – England Map in Tranquillity: Defining and Assessing a Valuable Resource*.

10 The focus of our gaze

1 Traherne, T. (2005) *The Kingdom of God* – Cap. 27, *The Works of Thomas Traherne*, ed. Jan Ross, Cambridge, D. S. Brewer, p. 400.

2 Traherne, *The Kingdom of God* – Cap. 27, p. 404.

3 Traherne, T. (2002) *Centuries* – C. I. 29 and 30, *Thomas Traherne: Poetry and Prose*, selected by Denise Inge, London, SPCK, p. 4.

4 Inge, J. (2003) *A Christian Theology of Place*, Aldershot, Ashgate, p. 76.

5 Irenaeus, *Adversus Haereses* IV, 28.

6 Blake, W. (1975) *Auguries of Innocence*, Burford, The Cygnet Press, p. 3.

7 Thomas, R. S. (2001) 'Pilgrimages', in *Collected Poems 1945–1990*, London, Phoenix Press, p. 364.

Copyright acknowledgements

Index